THOMAS WOLFE

Beyond
the Romantic Ego

TWENTIETH-CENTURY AMERICAN WRITERS

THOMAS WOLFE
Beyond
the Romantic Ego

by Leo Gurko

THOMAS Y. CROWELL COMPANY

New York

The quotation on pages 18 and 19 is from *Thomas Wolfe's Purdue Speech: "Writing and Living,"* edited by William Braswell and Leslie A. Field. Copyright © 1964 Purdue Research Foundation, West Lafayette, Indiana. Published by permission. Other quotations are from *Look Homeward, Angel, Of Time and the River, From Death to Morning,* and *The Story of a Novel* by Thomas Wolfe, published by Charles Scribner's Sons; *The Letters of Thomas Wolfe,* edited by Elizabeth Nowell, published by Charles Scribner's Sons; and *The Web and the Rock* and *You Can't Go Home Again* by Thomas Wolfe, published by Harper and Brothers. All quotations are protected by copyright and reprinted by permission.

Library of Congress Cataloging in Publication Data
Gurko, Leo.
Thomas Wolfe: beyond the romantic ego.
Bibliography: p.
Includes index.
    SUMMARY: A brief biography of the author, Thomas Wolfe, and an analysis of his works including *Look Homeward, Angel* and *You Can't Go Home Again.*
    1. Wolfe, Thomas, 1900–1938—Juv. lit. [1. Wolfe, Thomas, 1900–1938.   2. Authors, American]
I. Title.
PS3545.0337Z715 1975   813'.5'2[92]   74–34204
ISBN 0–690–00751–5
1 2 3 4 5 6 7 8 9 10

For
my students and colleagues
at Hofstra University

Contents

FOREWORD *1*

1 **An Ardent Life** *9*

2 *Look Homeward, Angel* *49*

3 *Of Time and the River* *79*

4 *The Web and the Rock* *108*

5 *You Can't Go Home Again* *137*

6 **Two Stories** *159*

7 **The Novelist Who Got Away** *168*

A SELECTED BIBLIOGRAPHY *177*

INDEX *181*

Foreword

꽃꽃 By the time Thomas Wolfe died in 1938, certain widely publicized judgments about him had already begun to harden into clichés. After several decades they have undergone little change. Here are some of them:

1. His novels are autobiographical, and he could not handle experiences that were not directly his own. He was therefore doomed to repeat himself endlessly. Eugene Gant and George Webber, the two heroes of his four novels, grow up in the same Southern town, have the same feelings of alienation, attend the same university, come North in search of fame and fortune as writers, and react to everything with the same kind of exaggerated emotional frenzy. In all this they are simply doing what Wolfe had done at the same stages in his own life. His early death, just weeks short of his thirty-eighth birthday, was surely a tragedy in personal terms, but it was not a tragedy in terms of his art since that art had nowhere to go except over its own well-worn track.

2. Emotionally he never developed beyond late adolescence. The key word in adolescence, as in childhood, is *I*, a pronoun to which Wolfe's writing remained totally loyal. The egotism of his young protagonists—overheated, hypersensitive, voracious—dominates the novels and forces them into its single restrictive channel. Their life aim is cosmic: to absorb totality, read all the books, travel over the entire earth, eat and drink in vast quantities, make love to all women, cram the whole world into themselves. Wolfe's favorite mythical figure is Faust, the man eager to sell his soul in exchange for the freedom to experience everything, and one of his favorite adjectives is "Faustian." This extreme longing for total life is the passion of youth, convinced that everything is possible, that there are no limits, that the universe will yield itself up to an outpouring of energy and will. This view predominating in Wolfe to the exclusion of all else, his works make their fundamental appeal to the reader at, say, seventeen. As the reader ages, matures, and passes beyond the magic orbit of his own youth, as other emotions and other considerations are aroused in him, the appeal dwindles. In later life Wolfe may seem no less a giant, but a giant more and more starkly and exclusively of adolescence.

William Styron, like so many others, went through this change of heart, and serves as a representative witness. After being overwhelmed by Wolfe at first reading, he goes on to explain what followed: "Years later, when I had come to my senses, I published a lengthy re-examination of Wolfe, during which I took the risk of saying that his unbearable prolixity, the naïveté of so many of his attitudes and insights, his intellectual virginity, his parochial and boyish heart, his inability to objectivize experience and thus create a believable ambience outside the narrow range of self—all of these

drastically reduced his importance as a writer with a se
claim on an adult mind."

3. His novels are not really works of art but loose
explosions of verbal energy. Wolfe kept detailed notebooks
and journals as he went along, and was forever jotting down
as usable material everything that occurred to him as soon as
it happened. So did Henry James and many another writer.
But where James planned, thought, dissected, discarded,
angled, and minutely shaped, Wolfe threw everything in,
confusing rawness with freshness, enthusiasm with spontaneity, energy with art. Read the chapters of any of his novels in
reverse order, so runs the argument, and their impact will
remain much the same.

Wolfe had no very clear sense of his novels as unified
works. Maxwell Perkins, his famous editor at Scribners, cut
out considerable chunks of the first novel and forced an
arbitrary ending to Wolfe's writing of the second. Novels
three and four were pieced together by Edward C. Aswell, a
second editor, out of a vast outpouring of manuscript left
behind by Wolfe at his death. They read less like novels than
like the raw material for novels, as though Wolfe were going
through all the gymnasium exercises for a fight without ever
getting to the fight itself. Hemingway once said of him: "He
was sad, really, like Carnera." Primo Carnera was a prize-
fighter of gigantic size and strength, who managed after a
fashion to become heavyweight champion. But he couldn't
punch and was humiliatingly beaten by smaller men. He
looked like a great fighter. He seemed to have all the
necessary qualifications, with a few special ones thrown in.
But it was all an illusion.

4. As a writer Wolfe is almost wholly derivative. The
feverish cultivation of his own genius and the abnormal

longing for fame he gets from Keats. Shelley supplies him with a passion for absolutes and, in the later novels, his growing interest in social reform. Even Wolfe's way of throwing himself burningly into every moment, even his dying young, link him to these Romantic poets. He is encouraged by Whitman both to swallow and regurgitate the cosmos. Mark Twain's instinct for the tall tale and his mining of frontier humor precede Wolfe's own movement along these lines. From James Joyce he learns the staccato effects, the verbal fragmentation, the vivid immediacy of stream of consciousness: extended passages in the style of *Ulysses* are scattered all through *Look Homeward, Angel*. Critics have swarmed for years over the yeasty landscape of Wolfe's writing, and traced entire skeinages of debt and influence. Not much room of his own has been left for the writer; even that room has been regarded as long on fervor and short on originality.

5. His dominant subject was the search for the lost father. Wolfe's heroes search furiously for a good many things: lane ends to heaven; doors that are forever closing on the edges of memory; wind-grieved ghosts that emerge and ebb in a translucent light; some vaguely Wordsworthian, prenatal paradise, intimations of which keep echoing in the remote reaches of the mind. But the established theory about all these quests is that their real goal is a powerful father figure. Wolfe's own father, W. O. Wolfe, and his fictional self in the early novels, Oliver Gant, were men of tremendous energy, potency, and magnetism, but ruined by illness, drunkenness, irresponsibility, gigantic defects of various kinds. They engendered in their sons the ideal image of the powerful father while lapsing from it themselves, and when they died, their roles unfulfilled, the void had to be filled by others.

There was George Pierce Baker, the renowned breeder of great playwrights, under whom Wolfe studied and to whom he attached himself in his three years at Harvard. Afterward came Maxwell Perkins, another older man of great presence and authority, who skillfully guided Wolfe into print and nurtured him through many of the emotional storms that followed. Even Wolfe's one celebrated love affair, with Aline Bernstein, which dominated the period between the departure of Professor Baker and the arrival of Max Perkins, has been read as a father fixation in a thinly disguised form. Almost twenty years older than Wolfe, an established set designer in the New York theatre, she provided him with as much guidance and counsel as sex. Confident, cheerful, secure in the world, she initiated him into the spheres of society, celebrity, and organized art within the great city, discharging the role of parent perhaps even more than that of mistress. Wolfe quarreled and parted from all these persons, yet the channeling of both life and work into the motif of the lost father was irresistibly established.

6. His one dimension is gigantism, and his novels are to be read as fervid obsessions with bulk, quantity, inflation—the outpourings of an outsized man. Wolfe was abnormally conscious of his own height and once wrote a short story, "Gulliver," on how it felt to be six feet six in a world filled with men who were five feet eight. His swollen perspective was encouraged by geography. The town in which he grew up—Asheville, North Carolina—was surrounded by a towering ring of mountains. The vast continental sprawl of the United States, with its huge rivers running on for hundreds of miles, its dizzying mountain ranges and divides, its seemingly endless space, became Wolfe's natural subject.

The well-publicized strain of gigantism in the American

character, in the American national experience, appealed to a similar strain in him. The Cyclops episode in *Ulysses*, with its calculated use of gigantism as a literary technique, was a model to embrace, as was the story of Gulliver among the Lilliputians. Swift, like Joyce, is frequently referred to in Wolfe, shoring up—if shoring up were needed—his natural inclination to quantify everything: emotions as well as physical objects. Those critics who found his novels irresistibly distasteful described them as classic cases of elephantiasis.

7. He was riddled with vicious prejudices. Jews and Negroes were his favorite targets, but he had enough hate left over to spray almost every immigrant ethnic group from Ireland to Slovakia. His bigotries were scarcely original: they were the stock brands of the Southern provincial. The Negroes are niggers who live in Niggertown and have their peculiar smell as well as their special color. The Jews are kikes and sheenies who live in plush Fifth Avenue apartments, are rich, powerful, and exotic, with ferociously sexual wives who specialize in seducing young Christian lads of unimpeachable purity and virtue.

Capping these currents of feeling was Wolfe's love affair with Germany, the country whose soul and spirit melded with his own in Wagnerian fusion. He was thoroughly at home in Nazi Germany. The Germans loved him, too. They translated his novels, bought them in large numbers, lionized him on his visits, and hailed him as the greatest American writer of the day. He in turn loved the singing and swilling in German beer halls, thrilled to the collective brotherhood exuding from the Germans in their mass gatherings at fairs, rallies, and parades, and conscious that his father's people had come from Germany, felt mystically at one with the

Germans. Later he became disillusioned with the Nazis. He developed feelings of admiration for the Jews. He even paid dramatic tribute to a potent and admirable Negro, Dick Prosser, during an explosive interlude in his third novel. Still, his racial albatross, as one critic called it, hung about his neck to the end.

8. Another, perhaps the most powerful of his obsessions was time. Time devoured reality and consigned it to the dead past. It could be brought back to life only through memory, but memory was limited and unreliable, so that much of our experience was doomed to be forgotten. Wolfe strained and sweated to remember. He struggled for total recall: "I would be sitting, for example, on the terrace of a café watching the flash and play of life before me on the Avenue de l'Opéra and suddenly I would remember the iron railing that goes along the boardwalk at Atlantic City. I could see it instantly just the way it was, the heavy iron pipe; its raw, galvanized look; the way the joints were fitted together. It was all so vivid and concrete that I could feel my hand upon it and know the exact dimensions, its size and weight and shape."

No fleeting or fugitive thought was too small for him to snatch at and pin down in his crowded notebooks. The frenzy of his prose was simply the mark of his agonizing effort to get hold of life before it vanished. Yet all the while he was seized by the sense of failure, that no matter how hard he tried a significant portion of everything would get away. Most human beings fear death as an unavoidable point in the future. Wolfe feared it as a remorseless movement into the past.

Like most clichés, these are to some extent true. They are also significantly false. Over the years, efforts have been made by various readers and critics to counter them by discovering in Wolfe quite different elements and qualities: he was, for example, not only a pantingly serious writer but a humorous one, too, with a striking gift for mimicry and parody, and even a penchant for just horsing around having undirected, mindless fun.

He could invent characters, like the part-Indian ballplayer Nebraska Crane in *The Web and the Rock*, who were not at all dependent on the immediate facts of his own life. Far from being limited to the narrative voice of his adolescent genius-heroes, he could turn out effective, even powerful pieces from someone else's point of view, like the aging Civil War veteran's in "Chickamauga" or the young girl's in "In The Park." To the charge of formlessness and lack of discipline, scores of instances of deliberate craftsmanship and conscious control have been summoned from his work. The range of his prejudices and bigotries was remarkable, but much more remarkable was his struggle to overcome them, a struggle that, whether successful or not, went on to the end of his life. And even his enslavement to time was being overcome by his growing awareness of the things in the world that were timeless—the phenomena of nature and the enduring emotions of men.

Very little of this, however, has taken effect. The original judgments formed about Wolfe, the early impressions left by his highly charged novels, have remained unchanged. I do not believe these judgments and impressions to be accurate. In any case, the time has come—as with every serious writer—for a fresh look at his achievement, as reflected in his life, personality, and art.

That is the purpose of my book.

1

An Ardent Life

〠〠 Thomas Wolfe was born in Asheville, North Carolina, on October 3, 1900, making his appearance with the new century. His parents, W. O. Wolfe and Julia Westall, had numerous children; of those who lived, Tom was the seventh and youngest. His father, a stonecutter specializing in tombstones, had migrated to the South from Pennsylvania. His mother was a local girl and his father's third wife. Their marriage was noisy, quarrelsome, profoundly unhappy, and monumentally dramatic—a source of endless tension and grief for the growing boy and of endless material for the future novelist.

It was a household full of personalities. The father loved to curse and shout, to declaim familiar passages from Shakespeare's plays and the standard English poems, and to conduct his daily life on the highest possible decibel level of noise and emotional energy. He was more interested in eating, drinking, and ranting than in earning a living or carrying on the grubby mundane responsibilities of family head, and he was far more interested in himself than in his wife and children. He had plenty of charm, vitality, and gusto, but he was really a big oversized baby and a great ham, one of those men-children who never grow up.

The mother also loved to talk; her voice was never still. Her tones were quieter but even more persistent than her husband's. His style resembled a waterfall's, rushing and booming all the time; she was like a creek that seems about to dry up at any moment but goes on and on into the endless distance. They were great talkers but bad listeners, so that their conversations never seemed to join but went on along parallel lines and at cross-purposes—a setup guaranteeing maximum misunderstanding and leading to specific quarrels that went on for days and an essential conflict that went on forever. So polarized were their personalities, so locked was each within the cage of his own ego that they soon swelled beyond life size and seemed to play out the mythical roles of the male and female figures in a play by Strindberg, more like forces in nature than the Mr. and Mrs. Wolfe who lived in a house on Woodfin Street, Asheville, North Carolina, and owned a marble shop in the town square.

There was a curious exchange between them of traditional roles. The father was indifferent to money, made a minimal living out of stonecutting without being absorbed in it. He was, instead, an enthusiastic cook and a passionate gardener; the huge meals he presided over at home were among the epic experiences of Wolfe's childhood. It was the mother who loved money, who pursued it with a ferocity that amounted to a lifelong fever. Buying, selling, and speculating in real estate were her favorite occupations; whatever cash she had went into lots, houses, land; perpetual buying and selling were all that could appease her rampant acquisitive instinct. This pathology also took the form of hoarding; she hated to throw anything away, however dilapidated or useless, and even kept for years bits and pieces of string. Finding her husband's improvidence and imprudence in money matters intolerable, she left his house when Tom was six and opened a boardinghouse on the next block, which she called the Old Kentucky Home. After that there were two establishments, with the father and the children commuting irregularly between them.

The mother also loved to travel, and often went off with the children, leaving the father behind. In 1904 she turned up at the World's Fair in St. Louis, where she operated a boardinghouse for months and where one of the boys, Grover, caught typhoid fever and died. She took the children to Florida several times, and in 1913 brought them to Washington to witness the inauguration of Woodrow Wilson. The father grumbled at this: he was a Republican and she a Democrat. They probably achieved the most exquisite political equilibrium in American history when they named their twin sons Grover Cleveland and Benjamin Harrison.

The father had his travel seizures, too. On one occasion he wandered all the way to California by himself. Domestically they followed different routes, yet never separated. It was in temperament that the cleavage was absolute. The father was a free outgoing spirit, craving air and space. The mother was a ground creature, burrowing into the earth and taking absolute root there, squirreling her resources while inching her way in all directions. They were both fierce centers of energy, in a state of almost perpetual opposition and collision.

The children also had their share of vividness. Frank, the

oldest boy, was a school dropout and soon developed into what in those days was called a ne'er-do-well. He sponged off his family, drifted away to the Middle West where he married a woman much older than himself and sponged off her, took to alcohol and drugs, and wound up in various sanitariums for varying lengths of time.

Mabel, next in age, played the role of substitute mother. She assumed charge of the father after Mrs. Wolfe left for the Old Kentucky Home. Blessed with liberal amounts of the family energy, she had a great capacity for taking care of other people. She nursed her father during his illnesses, sobered him up after his drunken binges, fed him, and still had time for her younger brothers stretching all the way down to Tom, ten years younger than herself. But Mabel was not a self-effacing, mousy creature going through life in a dim sacrificial spirit; she was aggressive, quick-tempered, often jeering, and as Henry James would say, tremendously there. She was also talented: she sang, played the piano, did vaudeville routines, and dreamed of becoming a professional entertainer. There was one other girl in the family, Effie, the oldest of the children. She married when very young and went to live in another state.

After Mabel came the twins, with their Presidential names. Grover died at twelve, but he made a strong enough impression upon his youngest brother to serve as the central figure of "The Lost Boy," one of Wolfe's greatest short stories. The other twin, Ben, grew up into an almost classic case of alienation: bitter, intelligent, ironic, frail of health, disillusioned with his parents and the family situation, and anxious to save Tom, in whom he took an unusual interest, from that situation in particular and the conventional world in general. He worked as a reporter for the town newspaper, the traditional haven for the cynical, the disillusioned, and the anguished of heart—and died young.

Still another brother, Fred, was Ben's opposite: cheerful, outgoing, genial of temper, despite the awesome burden of having to go through life with an incurable stammer. These sibling figures, together with the parents and the future author, appear in the novels and are given full-scale treatment. They got Wolfe off to a tremendous start, supplying him with a dramatic cast of characters, a ready-made network of complex relationships, and a complete set of thunderous emotions. In all of this he was not only an active participant but, as the very youngest in the family, an advantaged observer.

Of all the brothers and sisters, he was the most bookish. He began reading at a precociously early age and did so well in the beginning grades that his parents were persuaded to send him at the age of ten to a newly opened private school run by a Mr. and Mrs. Roberts. There was much grumbling over the money this cost, and some of the older children were jealous of Tom because family money was being spent on him and not on them. Mrs. Roberts, who had a passion for literature and a flair for spotting talent in her pupils, encouraged and sponsored him with great zeal. Figures like Mrs. Roberts appear in the lives of many writers: usually a teacher of English, usually female, without whose early interest and stimulating support life might very well have been different. Wolfe's relationship with her had a storybook quality—he admired her, called her the "mother of my spirit who fed me with light," remained grateful in later years, and poured his feelings out to her in letters long after he left Asheville.

xcept for a bitter interval when she grieved over the unflattering portrait of her husband in *Look Homeward, Angel*, the bond between them was undisturbed.

Wolfe grew up more intimately bound to his mother than his father. His mother breast-fed him until he was almost four, kept his hair in long curls until he was nine, and was loath to let him go. He lived with her in the Old Kentucky Home, shunted from room to room as paying guests arrived. When he wasn't going to school, reading, or wandering around town, he was selling subscriptions to the *Saturday Evening Post* door-to-door, running a paper route in the Negro section, maneuvering his father home from alcoholic stupors in local bars, and hustling trade for his mother's boardinghouse at the railroad station.

There was plenty of trade to be hustled. High up in the mountains, Asheville had a growing reputation as a health resort. It was a town when Wolfe was born, and a city by the time he left. A Vanderbilt had come down from the North and built a huge château in the French style a short distance out of town. A boom atmosphere had set in during Wolfe's boyhood, bringing with it money, growth, an increasing population, everything associated with "progress," but also bringing crowds, noise, boosterism, manic real-estate speculation, and the kind of money frenzy that was to make Asheville one of the most painful casualties of the great crash. In Wolfe's early impressionable years, the town's surge of expansion stimulated the expansive side of his own nature.

As a boy he was thin, awkward, excruciatingly tall, moody, given to explosive outbursts of energy followed by lapses into stupefying apathy. He felt himself to be different. Everyone does, of course. But with Wolfe, it was more than a feeling; it was a burning conviction. A conviction of this kind brings with it a sense of special destiny. When still very young, Wolfe was taken with this sense of special destiny, of some great role he was to play, some exalted function he would discharge. It was all vague and unformulated and did not obtrude into his conscious life, but it powerfully reinforced his awareness of himself and his separation from others. To these others, whether they loved him or not, it was plain that he was out of the ordinary, and it did not require a professional connoisseur of such matters like Mrs. Roberts to see that he had talent. He won a city-wide prize contest with an essay on Shakespeare. It was understood at an early point that he would go to college, the only one of his brothers and sisters to do so.

Tom wanted to go to the University of Virginia, the fashionable, upper-crust, glamour school of the South. But his father, nursing some vague hope that the boy would become a lawyer or politician and would profit from local contacts, insisted that he attend the state university at Chapel Hill, and he entered there as a freshman in September 1916, just short of his sixteenth birthday.

His four years at the University of North Carolina were a success by even the most conventional standards. He had no athletic ability and no social connections, but the college offered him plenty of chances to work along his own lines. He gravitated toward the weekly newspaper, *The Tar Heel*, first as a reporter, then as managing editor, then as editor-in-chief. He wrote poetry that appeared in the college literary monthly and plays that were put on by the college players. He became a big man on campus and was acclaimed as the class genius upon graduation. He ran into at least four professors who inspired him, and one of them, Frederick

Koch, who specialized in getting his students to write folk plays, encouraged him to go to Harvard, study under George Pierce Baker, his own former instructor, and perhaps become a playwright.

America entered the First World War in the spring of his freshman year, emptying the campus of draft-age upperclassmen. Wolfe was not only fiercely patriotic, like most young Southerners, but romantic about the war. He longed to enlist, and together with his contemporaries—Fitzgerald, Hemingway, Faulkner, Dos Passos—ached to get over to Europe and join in the great adventure. It was a severe disappointment when he did not make it. His eighteenth birthday was followed almost immediately by the Armistice, leaving him with a feeling of emptiness and anticlimax. He had marked time in school while, three thousand miles away, friends of his—even his own brother Fred, who had joined the navy— were taking part in what he considered the most splendid and serious drama of the age. The closest he got to the war was military drilling on the athletic fields where football had been suspended for the duration.

He spent one of his college summers clerking for his brother-in-law, a businessman whom Mabel had married. He spent a second working as a checker and timekeeper at the government installations at Norfolk, Virginia, and a third in his mother's boardinghouse where he had a serious—though platonic—love affair with a young woman five years older than himself who was spending a season in Asheville with an ailing small brother.

His undergraduate years were rendered somber by the growing and obviously incurable illness of his father, suffering from cancer. A college roommate died of a heart attack, shocking him profoundly. And the great flu epidemic of 1918 carried off one of the significant figures in Wolfe's imaginative life, Ben, Grover's twin, who had been rejected by the army earlier for reasons of health.

Wolfe was a striking and almost eccentrically recognizable figure on campus. He loped and shambled rather than walked. His hair was generally uncut, his clothes looked slept in, and he had already developed the bizarre living habits that were to engulf him in later life. He loved to prowl the streets at night and do his sleeping by day. He would occasionally leave his college quarters and register at hotels and rooming houses in nearby towns under the names of English poets like Samuel Taylor Coleridge and Thomas Chatterton, some famous, some obscure, as the mood seized him. He had a noisy wit, a gift for parody, and would burst into explosions of laughter startling even in a college crowd. And in obvious prefiguration of the way he would write his novels, he scribbled essays, editorials, bits of reportage, dialogue on whatever scraps of paper were at hand: the backs of envelopes, throwaways, the margins of brochures and printed pamphlets, even rolls of toilet paper. He was, in short, a "character," vivid, colorful, loud, very vulnerable to both hurt and praise, and wonderfully adolescent. People who knew him at Chapel Hill remembered him long after he left.

He roamed freely through the curriculum, read and wrote abundantly, talked a great deal, and thought occasionally, but when he graduated in June 1920, he had only the vaguest idea of what he wanted to do—or be. His only clear urge was to leave home, leave North Carolina and the South, and head for what seemed to him the dazzling Elysium of the North.

Among the Wolfes, the idea of Tom's going to Harvard was greeted with a chilling lack of enthusiasm. The father, now

lly ill, thought it a deplorable waste of time, when he
about it at all. The brothers and sisters resented the
project as a terrible squandering of the family money. The
mother, money-grubbing and practical, couldn't see that it
would lead anywhere. What was he preparing himself for,
after all? He didn't clearly know, couldn't exactly say. When
pressed, he would say he wanted to be a writer. A writer? In
the Asheville of 1920, that made as much sense as wanting to
be a polar explorer or an astronaut or a soldier of fortune.
Many years later, in a speech at Purdue University, Wolfe
explained what being a writer meant to someone like his
mother:

> A writer is first and foremost a working man. This may
> surprise you. It does surprise most people. For example,
> it has always surprised my mother, who is an admirable
> old woman, seventy-eight years old, who has worked all
> her life, as hard as any person of that age you know. But
> my mother, like so many other people, has never been
> able to get it into her head that writing is work. When I
> was home last summer, she said to me: "Now, boy, if
> you can get paid for doing the kind of thing you do,
> you're mighty lucky—for all the rest of your people had
> to *work* for a living!" I keep reminding her that writing
> is also work—as hard work, I think, as anyone can do—I
> keep insisting on the fact; and my mother amiably keeps
> agreeing. But also she keeps forgetting—and in un-
> guarded moments, I often get flashes of what is really
> going on in what the psychologists call her subcon-
> scious. And apparently, it is something like this: writing
> is a kind of stunt, a kind of trick which some people are
> born with—like being a sword-swallower . . . —and if
> one is fortunate enough to be born with this trick, or
> gift, he can, without much effort to himself, be paid for
> it.

I don't believe my mother's views upon the subject are at all extraordinary: in fact, I should say they represented, unconsciously at least, the views of a majority of people everywhere. I know my mother would certainly be surprised, and possibly astonished, if I told her that I thought I was a working man—by this, I mean a man who does actual hard physical labor—in very much the same way as my father was, who was a stonecutter; and if I told her that I looked upon the big room in which I work—with its crates of manuscript— its work-tables—its floor space—in very much the same way as my father looked upon his shop in which he had his tombstones, his big trestles, his mallets and chisels, and his blocks of granite—my mother would smile, but would consider my proposition as another fantastic flight of the imagination. And yet, it seems to me, it is not fantastic. . . . My own experience has been that a writer is, in every sense—particularly the physical one—a working man.

Since his mother did not understand what he was doing even after he succeeded at it, one can imagine her bewilderment before he began.

Everyone was against Tom's going North, except maybe to look for work. But more college? More book learning? And at the most expensive school in the country? Never. Absolutely not. But by this time Wolfe, like the other members of his family, was acutely responsive to the demands of his own personality. He had a driving and aggressive will. Whatever he thought he wanted, he would pursue to the end. Harvard had invaded his imagination, and he would storm heaven itself to get there. He threatened to leave, without a penny, and make his way no matter how. The argument continued, simmered, dragged on. At last his mother agreed to finance him for a year. She still secretly looked on him as a passionate extension of herself and ignored the loud protests of the others that she was favoring Tom at their expense.

His instinct for the grandiose was already highly visible. Whatever he longed for had to be the peak of its kind. The University of Virginia had been his early goal, the very zenith of Southern education. As a graduate student it was Harvard, the very zenith of American education, that magnetized him. And beyond Harvard lay New York, still to be reached and scaled, the greatest of cities, the "enfabled rock" that aroused his most vivid fantasies about success and fame. He came by this passion for the superlative honestly enough, in a straight line from his parents. In his wanderings his father had picked up a stone angel and installed it in his Asheville shop. He yearned to carve an angel himself—the summit, as he conceived it, of the stonecutter's art. He never did. The angel was somehow beyond him, but the idea of himself, a man, creating something divine was an aspiration typical of his outsized dreams. And the mother had what was for her an equivalent dream: getting hold of all the money in the world.

Wolfe spent three years at Harvard, for the most part writing dramas for Professor Baker's 47 Workshop. These works were energetic, long, loosely assembled, melodramatic, and good enough to be put on by the college players. Wolfe also developed an intimate relationship with the Widener Library at Harvard. He regarded its hundreds of thousands of books as a personal challenge, and threw himself into reading them as though they were the endless hordes of some enemy army. "I wander throughout the stacks of that great library there like some damned soul," he wrote to Mrs. Roberts, "never at rest—ever leaping ahead from the pages I read to thoughts of those I want to read."

He had the obscure conviction that living was a kind of

war, with a whole series of military redoubts to be stormed and taken. Or it presented itself as a series of obstacles, each higher than the one before, leading to some ultimate Himalayan pinnacle. When that was reached, then somehow the war, the whole human enterprise, life itself, would be won. The assault on the Widener Library, with the mental looting and sacking of its contents, was an early incident in Wolfe's assault upon the universe. He was not depressed or discouraged by the image of the world as an obstacle course. His response was exaltation.

In the years at Harvard three personalities impressed themselves upon him, and eventually made their way into *Of Time and the River.* One was his uncle Henry Westall (Bascom Pentland in the novel), who had migrated to Boston, gone to divinity school, been ordained as a Unitarian minister, then had given that up to become a real-estate operator. The grotesque fusion of God and Mammon in this figure so closely related to him by blood aroused Wolfe's imagination, as the more extreme and extravagantly colored human types were always to do. A second influential figure was, of course, George Pierce Baker (Professor Hatcher), one of the reigning gods in Wolfe's private pantheon, not because of any striking personal traits but for what appeared to be his mysterious, indeed awesome power to release the genius of budding playwrights and midwife their careers. Baker extracted a number of plays from his young Southern disciple, submitted them to extensive commentary and criticism, got them produced at Harvard, and encouraged Wolfe to try his luck on Broadway and become a professional playwright. This was certainly over and beyond the call of duty, though well within Baker's conception of his role in life.

Nothing would have pleased Wolfe more. After finally

receiving an M.A. in 1923, he went to New York in the summer of that year with letters of introduction to the Theater Guild and his most ambitious play securely in hand. But the Guild, after an interlude of several months, turned the play down, and with no visible or prospective means of support, Wolfe all but abandoned the theatre as a livelihood. He thought of teaching, but Baker was opposed, saying that it would dissipate his creative energies. Wolfe kept insisting that he had to eat, and Baker offered no hope in that direction. "I began to understand," he confided to Mrs. Roberts, "—a bitter draught it was—that Professor Baker was an excellent friend, a true critic, but a bad counsellor." Their relationship unraveled and came to an end, partly because of the insatiable demands of Wolfe's digestive tract, but partly because of his slowly growing conviction that he was not destined to be a playwright. When he parted company with Baker on that, it was plain there was nothing else of consequence for them to agree about.

The third Harvard personality who grew close to Wolfe was Kenneth Raisbeck (Francis Starwick in the novel). Though only two years Wolfe's senior, he was Professor Baker's assistant and exercised a kind of authority over the younger man that was a reflection of Baker's. He, too, had aspired to be a writer, but wound up an aesthete instead. He dressed like a dandy, knew all about restaurants and wines, affected a cultivated Eastern accent very different from his native Midwestern, was highly intelligent, and knew how to be charming. He was very impressive to Wolfe at first and very pathetic later. They were the kind of opposites that would naturally be drawn to one another. Raisbeck had polished manners and limited vitality. Wolfe's social surface was raw, but his creative energies were limitless. In the end, however, Wolfe was to develop a ferocious antipathy to aesthetes, book reviewers, literary critics, and college professors—those, he felt, who while incapable of creating anything themselves lived off the creative efforts of others. His intimacy with Raisbeck supplied him with the essential mold for this emotion.

The antipathy also revealed how thin-skinned he was, how vulnerable to the opinion of others. When his plays were criticized for whatever reason, he was not only upset but angry at the critics. He would attack them as stupid, philistine, insensitive, out of tune with true genius. Yet his anger, touched with paranoia, was equaled, even exceeded by his pain, humiliation, and hurt. He had a tremendous opinion of himself, accompanied, as so often happens, with a tremendous uncertainty. Any charge of incompetence or failure directed at him, any suggestion that his writing depended on the help or advice of editors and was not wholly under his own control, would at once depress him profoundly and trigger howls of outrage and indignation.

His novels are filled with caricatures of his critics, his letters with denunciation of *their* incompetence. Blessed—or burdened—with a combative temperament and a quivering vanity, he was doomed through life to waste ferocious sums of energy in endless skirmishes with a hostile world. His later years were marred by a series of lawsuits, involving such matters as the rights to his manuscripts and his use of real people as characters in his work. Characteristically he never wanted to compromise or settle out of court but to pursue each litigation to the absolute end, no matter what the cost. Vanity, disguising itself as a burning sense of justice, overcame prudence and rationality at every turn.

Whatever difficulties of temperament he had to contend with, there was still the unavoidable matter of how he was to earn a living. He had spent four years at the University of North Carolina at his father's expense, and three at Harvard with his mother paying most of the bills. His two college degrees were of no great help in launching him as a playwright, but they did qualify him for one profession: teaching. He did not want to teach, felt ill at ease at the thought of it, was convinced that teaching would injure his creative talent, and sent out letters of application to various departments of English with extreme reluctance.

He was offered a post at New York University for the spring and summer terms of 1924, which he accepted with mixed feelings. He was unsure of his aptitude as a teacher, but he was overjoyed at the prospect of living in New York. Armed with a seven-month contract for $1800, he settled down in a cheap room at the Hotel Albert, near Washington Square, and prepared for his new life. He continued to revise and rewrite his plays and continued to send them out to theatrical groups like the Provincetown Players. Months would pass before they would decide to reject the scripts, usually with generous praise and lists of proposed changes. The changes, even when made, did not bring acceptance, and the theatre as a prospective career began to fade. It was during this gray frustrating period in his creative life, when the impulse to write was more powerful than ever, that the idea of turning from drama to the novel took hold of his mind.

Meanwhile he had begun to teach. If his worst fears about himself as a teacher were not realized, it was only because he slaved at it and to some degree made up in energy and earnestness what he lacked in assurance and skill. He had three sections of freshman composition with more than a hundred students and the usual weekly themes. At these he sweated till all hours, correcting the endless mistakes in grammar and expression, annotating every page, pouring out his responses, and hating every minute of it. It took him away from his own writing and ate up his nervous resources. In class he fell back on reading aloud from the English poets, and did it with so much awkward eloquence, so much highly charged appreciation, that his students were oddly moved.

They were for the most part urban Jews, and as usual Wolfe was excessively conscious of them. Their dark foreign looks repelled him, yet he was sexually attracted to the females. The manifest intelligence and will to succeed of these Jewish students aroused his admiration. The intimate confrontation between them was dramatic, indeed almost stagey: the man-mountain of the young Protestant Southerner and the swarms of Semites one generation removed from the ghettos of Eastern Europe, facing each other in the great city that was their unexpected meeting ground.

Wolfe spent six years at N.Y.U., off and on. The school was unfailingly courteous and hospitable, granting him leaves of absence when he went abroad and welcoming him back on his return. He appears to have gotten along with his colleagues, his chairman, and the dean while there. It came as a cruel and unexpected shock to them to read his bitterly hostile account of the university in *Of Time and the River*, where Eugene Gant sneeringly refers to it as the School for Utility Cultures and speaks savagely of the faculty as a cabal of small-souled, self-seeking, backbiting figures obsessed with their sterile little promotions in the academic hierarchy.

After two terms of hard work at school, he saved up enough money for a European trip, and in October 1924 sailed on the first of his seven journeys abroad. It was a conventional grand tour through England, France, and Italy. In Paris he ran into Raisbeck and two young women from New England, and for a time the four of them traveled about together, with emotional complications that Wolfe was later to fictionalize in detail. At Harvard he had suspected Raisbeck of being a homosexual; now in France the homosexuality became blatant. There were scenes, shouts, quarrels, and a final blowup. Wolfe, who drank heavily throughout his life—a habit he shared with Fitzgerald, Hemingway, Faulkner, Sinclair Lewis, and Ring Lardner, prodigious boozers all—went on several extended drinking bouts during this troubled period. He had planned originally to return in February, but his mood changed, and he resolved to stay on in Europe. His money, however, ran out, and he had to plead with his mother for more funds. As always, they were forthcoming, though not without the usual angry grumbling back home. He had other small adventures in Europe, as well as those hundreds and thousands of minute daily impressions that relentlessly made their way into his notebooks.

In August 1925 he sailed for home, third class. In mid-ocean he ascended to a party given in second class, and there met the next of the decisive figures in his life: Mrs. Aline Bernstein, a wealthy, Jewish, New York theatrical designer, who had descended from first class to attend the party. If it was not exactly love at first sight, it was the next thing to it—a powerful attraction on each side. This was the second time Wolfe was to be in love, and the last. His crush on the young woman in his mother's boardinghouse had occurred when he was sixteen, and gone unconsummated. He had had brief sexual fruitions since and would continue to have them. But none of these other women meant anything to him emotionally; contacts with them were fugitive.

Aline Bernstein was not only the central figure in his love experience; she was the only woman with whom he had a complete relationship. She was the opposite of him in almost every respect, underlining once again the unrestrained drive in his nature for dramatic contrast. She was more than eighteen years his senior, old enough to be his mother as he never failed to remind her during their frequent quarrels. She had a son and daughter who were almost grown, and a rich stockbroker husband with whom she had a "friendly" understanding that she could do, live, and love as she pleased. She was short, round, and graceful in her movements, where Wolfe was very tall, thin at this time, and awkward. She was emotionally disciplined and self-controlled, thoroughly adjusted to the world around her—the world of the theatre, art, and fashionable society on the celebrity level. Wolfe was spasmodic, irregular in his habits, given to prolonged brooding, magnetized by his surroundings yet suspicious of them. She was good-natured, genial, affectionate, attuned. He was irascible, fractious, explosively passional, hungry.

In the fall of 1925 she persuaded him to give up his hotel room and rent a loft with her on East Eighth Street. There they began living together, and there, with her sympathetic encouragement, *Look Homeward, Angel* began to grow in his mind. The six years they spent together were certainly the rhapsodic climax of his life. He was at the height of his youthful energies. He had at last found the literary form suited to his powers after the theatrical blind alley in which he had vainly wandered. He was exploring and absorbing the great city in its greatest period during one of the glittering decades in American history.

Aline Bernstein was the catalyst in all this. She knew the theatre from the inside, recognized that Wolfe's talents lay elsewhere, and helped move him toward fiction. She knew the city in its upper reaches, gave parties which he attended, introduced him to everyone she knew, made him privy backstage to her activities as a theatrical designer. They roamed the streets of New York together and shared their impressions endlessly. He got her to talk about her childhood in the New York of the eighties and nineties where she had grown up as an actor's daughter; her recollections, like everything else Wolfe encountered, made their way into his work.

She was a splendid cook, and he loved to eat. She took care of his laundry, brought some semblance of order to his chaotic daily routine, and supplied in her cheerful presence a countervailing focus to his own dark, self-devouring temperament. Theirs was not one of the great love affairs of the ages, but neither Cleopatra nor Dido played as many roles as did Aline Bernstein. To be mistress, mother, sponsor, guide, and friendly companion to Thomas Wolfe for so long a time has to rank as one of the great feats in the history of love.

It was in the spring of 1926 that he began jotting down those recollections of his childhood that were to grow into his first novel. Impressed by them and believing in his genius, Aline proposed that he take a year off from teaching at her expense and devote himself to the book. They went to England in the summer of 1926, and he stayed on in the fall to work on the novel in earnest while she returned to New York. Their letters across the Atlantic began revealing the cracks and splits in their relationship that would eventually disintegrate it altogether. He was jealous of her returning to her theatrical commitments and resentful because she was supporting him. He was upset by her other life as a married woman, and the "half-beast" in him, as he called it, began clubbing her with insults about her age and her race. She, in turn, was upset by the sheer physical fact of their separation and was afraid that in her absence he would fall in love with someone else.

When he returned at the end of the year, however, they resumed as before. He spent the spring of 1927 on the book, and after another, this time brief, summer excursion to Europe with Aline, worked away on it without interruption when he started to teach again in the fall. They moved to larger quarters. His classes had been conveniently shifted to the evening, leaving his days free for the novel. Month after month of unremitting labor finally brought him in the spring of 1928 to the end. The manuscript was a colossus of almost four hundred thousand words. He called it *O Lost*, from the first two words of the refrain running through the novel: "O lost, and by the wind grieved, ghost, come back again."

This was to be discarded as a title for the book, but as an immediate reference to his life with Aline, it was prophetic. Finishing the novel appeared in some obscure way tied up with his mounting desire to be rid of her. He loved her, to be sure, but he hated her as well, and all her "defects" now seemed to him intolerable: her Jewishness, her age and partial deafness, her money on which he had been so humiliatingly dependent, her other life with husband and children, her worldly success which so far had evaded him, even her taking charge of his daily routine. He felt hemmed in, invaded by her, possessed. He now longed to shake free of her, exorcise her, and start afresh, unburdened by her dominating presence. Besides, he was profoundly convinced that his novel was great, and this revived his faith in himself and his genius, a growth of feeling that made his dependence on her repugnant.

The break between them did not happen all at once. There were more quarrels and more reconciliations. Aline sent the manuscript to several publishers, who rejected it on the grounds that it was too long, needed too many revisions, or was too radically new. She found an agent for him, Madeleine Boyd, who claimed she could not put the novel down once she began reading it. Almost without pausing for breath, Wolfe began writing a second novel while doubting that the first would ever get published. Getting published assumed the proportions of a miracle—remote and unattainable.

In the summer of 1928 he took still another leave of absence from N.Y.U. and went off to Europe again, this time alone. But there were long letters between him and Aline: his oscillated between wanting to make an end of it and wanting to make up in a renewal of passion; hers were all on a single note—she loved him and wanted to be with him forever; as for his coldness, she insisted it was just perversity on his part which, in his own best interests, he must conquer. He was in Munich in October, and while attending beer-hall festivities during the annual fair got drunk, struck a German, and in an ensuing brawl, wound up in a hospital with a broken nose and multiple lacerations of the scalp. But his wounds were eased when in Vienna, a month later, he received a note from Charles Scribner's Sons, to whom Mrs. Boyd had sent the book, praising it and asking him to see them as soon as he could. It was signed Maxwell E. Perkins. The name meant nothing to him; the letter, everything.

He was back in New York at the beginning of the new

year, 1929, and for once, despite the prospect of more teaching and the difficulties with Aline, was eager to return. He presented himself at Scribners on January second, and there met Perkins for the first time. Perkins had "discovered" Fitzgerald, collected and reissued the stories of Ring Lardner at a time when Lardner was considered a crude dialect humorist recording the antics of illiterate baseball players, and introduced Hemingway to American readers when he was virtually unknown. He had a genius for personal relationships and had become an intimate friend of all these writers. Now, as the twenties were drawing to a close, he was, at the age of forty-four, at the height of his influence and power as an editor. Yet his earlier experiences seemed only a preliminary, a kind of intricate rehearsal for the close involvement, the exhausting intensity, and the ultimate dissolution of his relationship with Wolfe.

Their first meeting was on Wolfe's side a tumultuous success, bordering, in his usual vein, on ecstasy. Perkins not only admired the novel; he wanted to publish it. He proposed that a section of it—"An Angel on the Porch"—be submitted for separate publication to *Scribner's Magazine* and offered Wolfe a contract and an advance. Of course, the manuscript was too long. The young author would, of course, be happy to reduce it. Perkins proposed deletions; Wolfe was only too eager to agree. He emerged from the Scribner building on Fifth Avenue, his heart pounding with excitement, his pulse racing at the thought of this triumphant breakthrough after all the years of effort and frustration. Without the slightest notion of what he was doing, he began walking north toward Harlem, instead of south toward his apartment where he was still being visited by Aline.

For three months he strained to shrink the size of *Look*

Homeward, Angel, a title he plucked from a line in Milton's "Lycidas" when Perkins suggested that he could do better than *O Lost*. His labor was fruitless. The more he worked at it, the more he revised, the more resistant the manuscript proved to reduction. But three hundred pages were finally eliminated, virtually all at Perkins's suggestion, and the novel was at last scheduled for publication in the fall.

Wolfe continued teaching through the spring and autumn, and continued working on his next novel. He and Aline were still together, though the strains were increasing. He wanted them to part, but he was not yet ready to make a final break, while the more anxious he was to separate, the more she clung to him. *Look Homeward, Angel*, with an eloquent dedication to her, came out in October. The personal copy that he gave her was inscribed as follows:

To Aline Bernstein

> On my 29th birthday, I present her with this, the first copy of my first book. This book was written because of her and is dedicated to her. At a time when my life seemed desolate, and when I had little faith in myself I met her. She brought me friendship, material and spiritual relief, and love such as I never had before. I hope therefore that readers of my book will find at least part of it worthy of such a woman.
>
> Thomas Wolfe
> Oct. 3, 1929.

It was the very month of the great stock-market crash, but as the American economy collapsed, Wolfe's stock soared spectacularly. The novel struck the literary world with singular force. The reviewers were enthusiastic. Readers, used to the restraints of Hemingway and the carefully controlled effects of Fitzgerald, were bowled over by the torrential energy, the rhetorical rush and luxuriance, the romantic outpouring of Wolfe. And though the autobiographical novel chronicling a young man's progress from birth to manhood was a stock item in literature, Wolfe's version of it had so much freshness and immediacy, re-created the town, the family, and the growing consciousness of Eugene Gant with such bold élan that *Look Homeward, Angel* seemed like something new of its kind.

Not only his book but Wolfe himself was brilliantly launched. He was hailed on all sides as the great new writer in American literature, an accolade climaxed the following year when Sinclair Lewis, in his speech accepting the Nobel Prize, singled him out for special praise. In the last months of 1929 and into 1930, he was something of a literary lion, invited to scores of parties, sought out by interviewers, pursued by women. He was awarded a Guggenheim Fellowship, and on the strength of it and the royalties from his book, resigned from N.Y.U. for good and all, and took off once again for Europe.

There he met F. Scott Fitzgerald for the first time, at a bad period in the older man's life. Zelda Fitzgerald had had her first breakdown. Fitzgerald's writing, after *The Great Gatsby*, had gone poorly, and he was drinking heavily. The two writers admired each other, but Wolfe refused to be drawn into Fitzgerald's Riviera life. He visited Germany again and had his first direct view of the Nazis, now—in 1930—visible not just in the beer halls but in the streets. He spent most of his time working on his second novel, whose early title *The October Fair* would eventually be changed to *Of Time and the River*. In London he met Sinclair Lewis, gaunt and ravaged-looking, whose generous public praise of *Look Homeward, Angel* Wolfe was never to forget.

He returned to the United States in 1931, and deadly serious now about spending his energies on his work without the distractions of parties and publicity, left Manhattan altogether and began living in Brooklyn. In Europe he had been followed by jealous letters from Aline. The dissolving relationship with Wolfe had begun to break her down. She attempted suicide; she wrote endless pleas for their coming together; she visited him in his apartment in Brooklyn and endured various humiliations and rejections—from his mother on one particularly painful occasion—all of which made her only the more desperately anxious to keep the affair alive. It was hopeless; at the beginning of 1932 they parted for good, and Wolfe was left free to concentrate on his work and pursue, without her continual presence, his dream of greatness.

The years in Brooklyn were marked by stubborn, punishing labor on his new book and severe harassment of spirit. *Look Homeward, Angel* had come out in England to a critical reception more mixed than in America, but in Germany it had been received with overwhelming acclaim. The American sales were modest, never producing quite enough royalties to meet Wolfe's living expenses, but what with the sale of an occasional story to the magazines—usually a chunk carved out of a novel in progress—and advances on future books, Wolfe managed to struggle along, though never easily or in comfort.

The one painful aspect of *Look Homeward, Angel* was the fury it aroused in Asheville. Almost everyone in town, from Mrs. Roberts on, claimed to recognize himself in one or another character in the novel and felt himself injured or demeaned. There was a general outcry against Wolfe as a scoundrel and an ingrate, and even threats against his person should he ever return. Asheville was badly hit by the collapse of the real-estate boom in the late twenties and by the depression that followed. Its mood was surly and despondent, and it found no comfort in Wolfe's savagely satirical chronicle of itself and its inhabitants.

Wolfe, convinced that he hadn't humiliated or muckraked anyone, that his characters had been radically altered by his imagination from the literal facts of life to the purposes of fiction, that he had indeed given them the kind of immortality that only art can bestow, was deeply upset by the uproar. He had gone back home during the twenties for brief visits; the ride on the train known as the K 19 from New York to Asheville was one of his favorites. But now he knew he could not return, that he was in truth banished from his native place, and he felt acutely injured. Years were to pass before feelings changed, and it was possible for him to go back.

Meanwhile the deliberate isolation of his life in Brooklyn was levying a heavy nervous toll upon him, though he was scarcely conscious of it at the time. There were literally weeks when he saw no one whom he really knew except the typist who came to type up the handwritten sheets profusely scattered in all directions, and Max Perkins, whom he saw at Scribners for lengthy, often wrenching discussions of the new book. He would frequently do his writing at night and prowl the streets of Brooklyn before dawn.

The worst years of the depression were now upon the country. The subways, alleys, doorways, were filled with derelicts, vagrants, and the unemployed unable to afford lodgings of their own and huddling together for refuge wherever they could. Brooklyn, he wrote to his English editor, "is a vast sprawl upon the face of the earth, which no man alive or dead has yet seen in its foul, dismal entirety. I don't know how it *looks* but I'm an authority on how it smells. In the subway . . . all these stinks have been mixed, melted, fused and wrought into one glamorous, nauseating whole—and *that* is the way Brooklyn smells."

Wolfe's social consciousness erupted at this time. He had always been vaguely liberal, with standard, hand-me-down opinions about American materialism. His mother's real-estate speculations had seemed to him dreadful, and though he was not sentimental about the evils of money, the moneyed life of the middle class repelled him. Yet he had lived through the twenties scarcely concerned and hardly aware of what was going on around him. The thirties, however, with their calamitous misfortunes vividly embodied in the suffering men all about him during his four years in Brooklyn, finally got through to him and turned him into an aroused, aggressive humanitarian. He would indeed come to find Perkins's ingrained conservatism repugnant—an ideological split that turned out to be one of the grounds for their ultimate separation.

But whatever his concern for the general human welfare, he was in many ways indifferent and abusive to his own. His diet consisted of huge quantities of coffee, liquor, and cigarettes, with meals consumed in irregular quantities at irregular hours. "Doing a book is agony—60 cigarettes a day, 20 cups of coffee, miles of walking and flinging about, nightmares, nerves, madness—there are better ways, but this, God help me, is mine." He began putting on weight and developed a bald spot. But while his looks declined, while the image of the romantic youth began to fade, his creative energies, his fantastic productivity, showed no signs of abating. *Of Time and the River,* in manuscript, ballooned to seven hundred thousand words, aptly illustrating Wolfe's own metaphor for the creative process:

> I had inside me, swelling and gathering all the time, a huge black cloud . . . loaded with electricity, pregnant, crested, with a kind of hurricane violence that could not be held in check. . . . I cannot really say the book was written. It was something that took hold of me and possessed me. . . . It was exactly as if this great black storm cloud . . . had opened up and, mid flashes of lightning, was pouring from its depth a torrential and ungovernable flood. Upon that flood everything was swept and borne along as by a great river. And I was borne along with it.

Getting the book down to publishable size put Wolfe's relationship with Perkins under unbearable strain. Perkins was anxious for a second novel to appear as soon as possible, to take advantage of the success achieved by *Look Homeward, Angel* and the stir it had created. Years passed, however, and Wolfe showed no signs of finishing. He had begun with vast sweeps through the early history of his family three and four generations back. Yet these sweeps never came to a climax but only disappeared into the endless underbrush of history.

At last he gave most of this up and settled down to the further experiences of Eugene Gant, at Harvard and in Europe. But even this relatively straightforward story line led to no visible resolution, seemed to go on and on toward some remote horizon. Author and editor, now the closest friends, struggled for a beginning, middle, and end to the book, but though there was absolute goodwill on both sides, they could not agree. Wolfe wanted to go on writing until his novel achieved its form; other considerations were secondary. It was now 1934, and Perkins finally decided that left to himself Wolfe would never be satisfied, that he would simply go on forever. In Wolfe's own interest—as well as in Scribners'— Perkins opted for an arbitrary cutoff point, and almost without Wolfe being fully aware of it, sent the manuscript to the printer.

Reading the galleys increased Wolfe's uneasiness about the novel. He lamented that he hadn't been given another six months in which to finish it, and felt, paraphrasing Shakespeare, that "it had been from his womb untimely ripped." Still, it ran to more than nine hundred pages in its printed form, impressing even Wolfe with what he had accomplished and stimulating in him, side by side with his dissatisfaction, an immense welling up of gratitude to Perkins for his unceasing and devoted labors. The novel came out in the spring of 1935. By then Wolfe had closed up his Brooklyn quarters for good, stuffed his several million written but unpublished words into wooden packing cases, which he left with Perkins, and taken off again for Europe.

While in England he learned, with mingled surprise and pleasure, that *Of Time and the River* was being reviewed enthusiastically and was selling more briskly than *Look Homeward, Angel*. Buoyed up by this welcome news, he went to Germany where in a congenial atmosphere of adulation by the Germans and his own feeling of at homeness, he was as yet only dimly aware of the grimmer aspects of Nazism, now in its third year in power. In July he was back again in New York, enjoying the success of his second novel and his widening fame. That summer he accepted an invitation to address a writers' conference at the University of Colorado; after it was over, he spent a number of weeks touring the

West. The fantastic landscapes stretching from New Mexico to California extracted from him almost glandular bursts of enthusiasm, and supplied him with the physical frame for a six-novel epic he was planning about America from its beginning.

This was a typical enterprise for Wolfe: vast, sweeping, covering the whole of history and the whole of geography, providing him with the infinite imaginative space in which his hunger to describe and express everything could roam about at will. Again he wrote long swatches of this ambitious work, and again it remained unfocused, in the grip of an obscurely powerful centrifugal force that kept pulling it away from its uncreated and perhaps uncreatable center. Again Wolfe was forced to give it up and return to the immediate experiences of his more or less contemporary heroes. He had lost interest in Eugene Gant and started on a new protagonist named George Webber, the pivotal figure in novels three and four. Fragments of his American epic eventually turned up in these books, but most of the hundreds of thousands of words it had extracted from him found their way into the packing cases that made up the bulk of his estate on his death.

In the fall of 1935 he was back from his Western trip and living again in Manhattan, this time in a comfortable apartment overlooking the East River. Now that he was past the psychological roadblock of a second novel, the future seemed clear. This soon proved to be an illusion.

The remarks in his Colorado speech were expanded into a little book of nonfiction, *The Story of a Novel*, recounting Wolfe's experiences in writing *Of Time and the River*. But its publication led to a nagging dispute with Scribners over royalties. At this time, too, Bernard De Voto produced his famous attack on Wolfe in an article called "Genius Is Not

Enough." He accused Wolfe of being utterly dependent on Scribners' "assembly-line," without which he could never have gotten his novels out at all. This charge had a surface plausibility but was essentially untrue, as Wolfe tried to convince himself by recalling that he had written and finished *Look Homeward, Angel* before ever meeting Perkins or having anything to do with Scribners. Still, De Voto's words broke through his thin skin and injured him severely. Perkins was, of course, a tower of strength, but perhaps the time had come to prove to the De Votos of the world—and in some obscure way to himself as well—that he could function without Perkins, that he, Wolfe, was in truth the sole creator and owner of the works appearing under his name.

These rifts and tensions were exacerbated by the lawsuits in which Wolfe became entangled. After leaving Brooklyn he had published a collection of stories, *From Death to Morning*. One of his Brooklyn landladies claimed that she had been libeled in these stories, and was suing author and publisher for damages. Wolfe had parted company with Madeleine Boyd, his first agent, but she was demanding fees that she claimed he owed her for the translated editions of *Look Homeward, Angel*. Some years before, Wolfe had given a young book dealer the right to sell the manuscripts of his novels. He had canceled this oral agreement, and was being dunned by the dealer for money on the ground that his professional reputation had been damaged by Wolfe's repudiation of him. Wolfe responded by suing him for the return of the unsold manuscripts still in his possession. In all these disputes Wolfe felt that Scribners was giving him bad advice, urging him to settle and pay up while his inclination was to fight to the end.

Other disputes cropped up. Scribners was slow to offer him

a contract for his next book, and Wolfe was aggrieved.
Perkins learned that Wolfe was planning to write about
Scribners as a firm and about the people employed there,
including naturally Perkins himself. Perkins did not object to
himself as a character in Wolfe's fiction, but he strenuously
objected to Wolfe's exploiting his associates, using details
that Perkins had told him in confidence. This made Wolfe
very angry. Perkins had had no objection, he argued, to
Wolfe's "exploiting" his own family and the people of
Asheville in *Look Homeward, Angel,* or the assorted figures at
Harvard in *Of Time and the River.* It was only when Perkins's
own turf was threatened that he got up on his high horse.
Wolfe was determined not to be ruled by this kind of double
standard. He would write as he pleased, unmoved by
Perkins's attempts at censorship.

Their disagreements festered, smoldered, and grew more
heated during 1936. In the summer Wolfe returned to
Germany and attended the Olympic Games. The story goes
that when Jesse Owens, the black runner, won the sprints
Wolfe let out a shout of joy, which caused Hitler to turn his
head and glare. It was during this visit that Wolfe's active
disillusionment with the Nazis set in. Their brutality and
fanaticism, their harsh treatment of the Jews, began at last to
register with him, and caused him to suspect that there was
some hidden disease in the German soul, surfacing now so
plainly that even he, with his hitherto blind feeling of
intimacy and oneness with the German people, was violently
repelled.

As his politics became more liberal, he associated himself
more and more with "suffering humanity." He had escorted
his mother to Roosevelt's first inauguration in 1933, and his
enthusiasm for the New Deal sharpened his ideological

differences with Perkins. Perkins distrusted FDR and disliked his avid concentration of power in the federal government. Like most conservatives, he felt that the world would be improved—if it could be improved at all—by personal example and individual action rather than by social and political legislation or government decree. He was not, however, disposed to argue these matters. Wolfe was. Where Perkins's conservatism was muted and restrained, Wolfe's liberal views, now rapidly developing into an undifferentiated kind of romantic radicalism, were voluble and insistent. It was not enough that *he* believed as he did; he felt compelled to proselytize Perkins. He failed, and the failure filled him with dismay.

Yet even as his quarrel with Scribners was approaching its climax in 1937, he was writing more furiously and productively than ever. After several starts in other directions, after various changes of title, the novels that were to be published after his death as *The Web and the Rock* and *You Can't Go Home Again* were now under way. He gave up his apartment and went back to living in hotels, settling finally in an eighth-floor suite of rooms in the Hotel Chelsea, on Twenty-third Street—destined to be his last address. He had also changed literary agents, and his new one, Elizabeth Nowell, helped him through the difficult period when he finally left Scribners and cast about for a new publisher. By the end of 1937 he found one in Harper's, and with it a new editor, a sympathetic young Southerner named Edward C. Aswell.

He began the last year of his life—1938—on a high plateau of personal prosperity and creative fulfillment. He had established new connections and relationships necessary to his peace of mind while not altogether giving up the old ones. Perkins remained his friend, and was in fact designated in his will as his literary executor. He had gone back and made his peace with Asheville, living in a rented cabin a few miles out of town in the summer of 1937, working as steadily as he could, though pestered by more visitors than he was in the mood for. He had enough material to work on to feed his art and enough public admiration and acclaim to feed his vanity. He accepted an invitation to speak at still another college, this time Purdue University, in May 1938. He did not fancy himself a public speaker. Such occasions made him nervous. He stammered. But he liked doing it, and simply dipped into his endless supply of personal experiences as a writer to keep him going. And the fee of three hundred dollars offered him by the school fattened his exchequer agreeably. His remarks at Purdue had more political and social content than his talk at Colorado three years before, a measure of how much he had been drawn outward into the stream of history. And as before, he seized the occasion, after the speech was delivered, to explore a part of the country he had never been to—the Northwest.

He spent the early summer pounding along by car through vast stretches of territory from the Grand Canyon and the Mojave Desert to Mount Rainier. At the beginning of July he was in Seattle, and on the Fourth left by boat for a short excursion to British Columbia. On this journey he shared a bottle of whiskey with a fellow passenger who came down with influenza, and Wolfe upon arriving at Vancouver was running a fever. Having come that far, however, he persisted in going about and seeing the sights. But the illness increased, and he was forced to take a train back to Seattle, getting progressively worse all the way there.

For a week he lay in his hotel room unattended. He was at last persuaded by friends to enter a hospital, and there, at the other end of the country, his fatal illness began running its final course. He had pneumonia, and was at the same time suffering from violent headaches. His sister Mabel arrived from the East to look after him. The pneumonia was at last brought under control, but the headaches persisted and grew worse, and he was advised by the attending doctors to make the admittedly taxing journey to Baltimore for the more expert treatment he would get at Johns Hopkins.

While still in the hospital at Seattle, he sent on August twelfth an extraordinary letter to Perkins, the last letter of his life:

> I've made a long voyage and been to a strange country, and I've seen the dark man very close; and I don't think I was too much afraid of him, but so much of mortality still clings to me—I wanted most desperately to live and still do . . . and there was the impossible anguish and regret of all the work I had not done, of all the work I had to do—and I know now I'm just a grain of dust, and I feel as if a great window has been opened on life I did not know about before. . . .
>
> Whatever happens—I had this "hunch" and wanted to write you and tell you, no matter what happens or has happened, I shall always think of you and feel about you the way it was that Fourth of July day three years ago when you met me at the boat, and we went out on the café on the river and had a drink and later went on top of the tall building, and all the strangeness and the glory and the power of life and of the city was below.

Attended by Mabel, he embarked on the arduous, debilitating, three-day train trip across the continent. In Baltimore his mother was waiting for him, and so were the surgeons and specialists at Johns Hopkins. An exploratory brain operation to discover the cause of the headaches was proposed. The surgeon performing it took one look at Wolfe's brain, saw that it was overrun with tubercle bacilli, and realized the case was hopeless. A tubercular lung lesion, healed in his boyhood long ago, had apparently been opened by the pneumonia, releasing the bacilli into the bloodstream and thence, fatally, to the brain. There was nothing to do but wait for the end. It came on September fifteenth, in the very city and almost in the very place where Wolfe's father had died the decade before.

Wolfe was buried in the family plot in Asheville, surrounded by the graves of his father and twin brothers, Grover and Ben. On his tombstone appear two inscriptions, taken from his novels: "The last voyage, the longest, the best," from *Look Homeward, Angel*; "Death bent to touch his chosen son with mercy, love and pity, and put the seal of honor on him when he died," from *The Web and the Rock*. With this, the turbulent, feverishly consummated life of an American original came to a close.

No matter how one "interprets" the life and personality of Thomas Wolfe, the result is satisfying. From a Darwinian standpoint, he was certainly a complex organism struggling for self-realization: moving from South to North, he adjusted to a profound change of environment and progressed with instinctive dynamism toward achieving higher forms of himself. The Freudians could find enough Oedipal connections with father and mother, enough sibling rivalries and tensions with his brothers and sisters, enough evidence in his work of slow, painful movement from id toward superego, to flesh out a volume.

Cultural-historical critics would have no trouble explaining Wolfe as a phenomenon peculiar to America: the country boy who makes good in the big city; the Horatio Alger figure whose origins are modest but who by dint of hard work, determination, pluck, and refusal to be discouraged in the face of adversity rises to the top; the outsized figure whose dimensions reflect the hugeness of the continent, whose explosive energy is a symbol of its enormous vitality, who embodies in actuality the mythic traits of folk heroes like Paul Bunyan and John Henry, traits geared to accomplishments of epic bulk. He is the American convinced that everything is possible, that human beings can dominate circumstances, that the world can be conquered, and the achievement of success is largely a matter of willing it—all in contrast to the European view that man is finite, life is limited, the gap between aspiration and achievement unspannable, and circumstances visibly more powerful than individual will.

Pragmatic critics, rooted to the immediate time and place, would find the three major periods lived through by Wolfe ripe sources for the revelation of both his conduct and his self. He had grown up among the late Victorian proprieties of the years before the First World War. His own twenties had run parallel with the 1920s when the settled values of the nineteenth century had gone through a feverish breakup. The crash of the stock market had ushered in the depression and the New Deal; the awakened individual consciousness of the twenties was replaced by the awakened social consciousness of the thirties. Wolfe had grown up under the restraints of the prewar era, nourishing his own individuality as best he could, encouraged by his brother Ben not to let "them" bear him down. When he left home, the war was over, the country was entering the Great Boom, and Wolfe exploded outward together with it; at Harvard, in New York and Europe, he lived an intensely liberated life in terms of art, love, and freedom of action, cultivating his energies, powers, and personality for all they were worth. His own ideological attachment to others, his feeling of solidarity with mankind, particularly oppressed mankind, did not come upon him until the thirties.

These changes and progressions are read into his novels. The first, *Look Homeward, Angel*, deals entirely with the early period, just before the First World War. The next novel, *Of Time and the River*, takes place in the succeeding period, the twenties. The third novel, *The Web and the Rock*, shuttles back and forth between the two. The fourth and last novel, *You Can't Go Home Again*, is entirely a book of the thirties. Thus, in terms of specific time and place, Wolfe's life as well as work can and, according to this school of interpreters, should be read as an illuminating record of the era in which he was brought up and to which he immediately belonged. From this standpoint no deep-think psychology, no long-range cultural analysis, are needed to reveal what is made perfectly plain by the surface facts.

In any case Wolfe lives up to our expectation of what the artist should be: like everybody else only more so, with the same traits present in the rest of us heightened and intensified, even exaggerated to the point of maximum visibility. Most of what was visible was of no special interest. His Southern bigotries, his ethnic prejudices, the liberal opinions and humanitarian attachments of his later years, were in themselves conventionally familiar, even stock. Wolfe was an obviously intelligent man but not unusually so; his mind showed no signs of profundity or distinction. His experiences as a son were uncommonly vivid, but there was little in his activities as student, teacher, lover, traveler, or worldling to make them memorable. His compulsive energy lent everything he did an extraordinary vigor and coloration, yet aside from this picturesque element nearly everything he did was reasonably familiar.

In one supreme respect, however, his life stands out, like a nunatak thrusting above the surface of a glacier. He had a remarkable vision of greatness, his own greatness to be sure, but of epic intensity and grain nonetheless. It took the form of the art ideal—Wolfe had called the artist "life's strongest man, earth's greatest hero"—but art conceived as nothing less than the seizing and defining of the whole human enterprise. In a famous letter to Fitzgerald, Wolfe announced himself a "putter-inner," not a "taker-outer." He wanted to put in everything. Though he did not succeed, though his art was supported at every point by a colossal vanity, there was something formidable about his conception of imaginative literature as a total encompassment of reality.

Whatever this did for his art, it gave his life its note of authentic exaltation.

2

Look Homeward, Angel

꒜꒜ Wolfe's first novel is perhaps his most famous work, and
certainly the most widely read. Many first novels, especially
when their authors are very young, tend to be heavily
autobiographical. *Look Homeward, Angel* is more so than
most. It covers the first twenty years in the life of its hero,
Eugene Gant, and these years follow, with an almost
unswerving literalness, the same period in the life of Wolfe
himself.

The title of the novel is one of its eloquent features. The
act of looking homeward suggests the main current of the
book. It evokes nostalgia and hints at illumination. Perhaps in
going back in mind and memory to the beginning of things,
we may discover what it is all about.

And it is an angel, not just a man, who is being urged to
look homeward. This transcendent note is essential to Wolfe's
purpose. It is not only man but the universe as a whole

being brought into the field of discourse. The title comes from "Lycidas," which ends with Milton's drowned friend placed in a focus greater than the narrow frame of mortality. The operations not merely of an individual life but the world at large are what ultimately concern Wolfe: in a letter to Sherwood Anderson, he refers to "my death-defying duel with the universe." The two generations of the Gant family chronicled in the novel are only dramatic illustrations of a process infinitely larger and more extensive than themselves.

The book has a subtitle: *A Story of the Buried Life*. This is as intriguing as the title, and draws our attention away from the cosmic toward the personal, from the world outside to the world within—the mind and soul of Eugene Gant, as it turns out. Wolfe feels compelled to get both dimensions in, true to his dramatic sense of encompassing the extremes.

After the title page, we are not admitted at once into Chapter One. Other items intervene. First comes the dedication to Aline Bernstein, supported by an appropriately ardent quotation from a poem by Donne. This is followed by Wolfe's statement "To the Reader," which turns out to be an elaboration of the familiar reminder in works of fiction that the characters are purely fictitious and any resemblance between them and actual persons is wholly coincidental. After all, says Wolfe, taking up in advance one of the accusations against him he was to find most nagging, all fiction is autobiographical and "a novelist may turn over half the people in a town to make a single figure in his novel." No doubt, but the people in Asheville seemed to have had no trouble picking themselves out. This may not invalidate Wolfe's argument but only indicate that he didn't do enough "turning over" to hide the face of raw actual life.

Finally, there is the epigraph, perhaps the most famous of

his career, which is used as a refrain throughout the novel. It begins with "a stone, a leaf, an unfound door" and ends with "O lost, and by the wind grieved, ghost, come back again." But its best section, one of many brilliant moments in Wolfe, is the following:

> Naked and alone we came into exile. In her dark womb we did not know our mother's face; from the prison of her flesh have we come into the unspeakable and incommunicable prison of this earth.
>
> Which of us has known his brother? Which of us has looked into his father's heart? Which of us has not remained forever prison-pent? Which of us is not forever a stranger and alone?

There is nothing strikingly original, or even fresh, about these rhetorical questions. That human beings have trouble communicating with each other is a general conviction that goes back a long way. Stripped of the rhetoric in which Wolfe clothes these familiar sentiments, they border on truisms. Yet it is a sign of the powerful energy of his novel that he manages to invest them with revealing eloquence and terrific force. The language conveying them is so radiant and splendid that we are left with the impression not of how familiar they are but that we are hearing them for the first time.

After all these preliminaries, the novel is ready to begin, and we run into something dazzling almost at once: the second and third paragraphs, surely among the great statements in modern literature.

> Each of us is all the sums he has not counted: subtract us into nakedness and night again, and you shall see begin in Crete four thousand years ago the love that ended yesterday in Texas.

> The seed of our destruction will blossom in the
> desert, the alexin of our cure grows by a mountain rock,
> and our lives are haunted by a Georgia slattern, because
> a London cutpurse went unhung. Each moment is the
> fruit of forty thousand years. The minute-winning days,
> like flies, buzz home to death, and every moment is a
> window on all time.

One of his great strengths as a writer lies here: his extraordinary capacity to link us with something larger than ourselves,
to splice the immediate, instantaneous present into a seamless
union with the all but endless past. He now takes one such
moment and uses it as a window on the time of the novel: the
hero's grandfather emigrates from England and settles among
the Pennsylvania Dutch. This event launches *Look Homeward, Angel* on the personal side; and with it the two
persistent dimensions in Wolfe—the cosmic and the immediate, the past and the present, the whole human race and a
cluster of individual characters, what endures forever and
what lasts for a transient moment—are announced. All this
on the very first page of the very first novel. No operatic
overture introduced its principal themes more swiftly or
persuasively.

Before the birth of the hero, there is the father, whose life
is given a full-scale treatment. The technique here, which
Wolfe will use more intensively in his later writing, is to
relate the father to events and processes larger than himself
and thus define him not just in terms of himself but in terms
of the universe. At twelve he stands by the roadside and
watches Lee's army march toward Gettysburg, tying him at
first hand to the larger movements of American history. On
his haphazard wanderings southward he stops off in Baltimore, learns the stonecutter's trade, and picks up a stone

angel: this sculptured figure, though a poor example of its kind, becomes an object he obsessively longs to reproduce. Having been linked at Gettysburg with history, he is linked in Baltimore with art.

His greatest role is yet to come, that of father. In the Blue Ridge Mountains of North Carolina he begets his numerous children, the last of whom turns out to be the most remarkable, almost by way of underlining Oliver Gant's phenomenal energy. His aggressive fatherhood establishes him as a biological force. His potency with food and gardens, with the process of growing things, the ferocious vitality with which he carries on everything he does, establish him not just as an individual man but as an element in nature.

He thus serves as an early example, in these deliberately cultivated liaisons with history, art, and nature, of Wolfe's favorite habit of presenting his major figures in a double focus, as individuals and as universals. Just as D. H. Lawrence's characters are not intended to be taken as personalities traditionally conceived but as separate fields of psychic energy, so the figures in Wolfe—beginning with the four principals in *Look Homeward, Angel*, Oliver and Eliza Gant and two of their sons, Ben and Eugene—are to be read as clusters of cosmic force, embodying something larger than their own selves.

Yet Oliver Gant, for all his vitality, is a mindless drifter who lives only in the moment. He is a force in nature to be sure, but that aspect of nature that lives, breathes, generates, in the here and now with little recollection of the past and no thought of the future. He wanders from city to city, from region to region, for no reason other than a vague restlessness. He drifts to the South, and marries a Southern girl, Eliza Pentland, as unselectively as he had married twice before.

The marriage is unhappy, yet he is doomed by circumstances, by the many children, by the burden of domesticity, to settle down in Altamont, where he feels himself a stranger among the Southerners and in deadly conflict with his wife.

He wants to drink, eat, make love, and spend everything he has to gratify immediate appetites. She is against liquor, eats very little, has had enough of lovemaking, and lives only to accumulate money and property. She incarnates that part of nature which ignores the present and exists only for the future. The clash between husband and wife is irreconcilable; their tragedy is that they both lose, and both are aware of it. The man especially so:

> Gant, faced with the loss of sensuous delight, knowing the time had come when all his . . . eating, drinking and loving must come under the halter, knew of no gain that could compensate him for the loss. . . . He felt, more than ever, the strangeness and loneliness of our little adventure upon the earth: he thought of his childhood on the Dutch farm, the Baltimore days, the aimless drift down the continent, the appalling fixation of his whole life upon a series of accidents. The enormous tragedy of accident hung like a gray cloud over his life. He saw more clearly than ever that he was a stranger in a strange land among people who would always be alien to him. Strangest of all, he thought, was this union, by which he had begotten children, created a life dependent on him, with a woman so remote from all he understood.

The woman, though deeply injured, continues her deadly pursuit of money; the future after all is a far larger arena than the present. Gant, the present denied him, his spontaneous impulses checked, takes refuge in erratic and humiliating bouts of drunkenness, in cursing and ranting, and slowly

subsides, like a wrecked ship, into a vast, soothing, stupefying
sea of self-pity. All this is described with splendor, vividness,
and absolute conviction. The earlier generation thus defined,
the domestic drama clearly set, we are at last brought to the
year 1900, the first year of the new century that witnessed
not only the birth of the author but the advent of his first
hero, Eugene Gant.

He is delivered by a doctor named Cardiac, but we must
not hold that against him. Wolfe had read too many plays by
Jonson and Congreve, where characters are named after
traits or occupations, and his imitation of these early devices
is sometimes crude. We are informed at once that while
Eugene means "well born," it does not mean "well bred." If
this distinction escaped us during the earlier chronicle of his
parents, it is not likely to do so in the account of the family in
which he grows up.

But Wolfe is not yet through setting the stage. The birth of
a hero is an awesome event, but since he first appears as a
squawling, helpless infant, this has its ridiculous side. And
Wolfe, who had a flair for parody and broad satire, introduces
the ridiculous side with two light strokes. He mocks conventional expectations at the birth of a boy, calling Eugene "the
complete male in miniature, the tiny acorn from which the
mighty oak must grow, the heir of all the ages."

We are then brought up to date on what has happened to
the rest of the world by 1900 with a wonderfully funny page
of monumental trivia: a Halifax Fisheries Award of
$5,500,000 to Britain for twelve-year-old fishing privileges,
Japan's first parliament meeting in 1891, Belisarius blinded
by Justinian, Hippias expelled from Athens by the Alcaemon-
idae, and a catalogue of other comically irrelevant events.

Wolfe is deriding the pedantic tendency to see everything "in depth." His humor is always expressive though not always reliable, but even when unreliable it serves a vital purpose in his writing: it supplies a badly needed leaven of deflation to an art that lists heavily in the opposite direction.

Eugene is in the world at last, ushered in with plenty of style. He now has to go through the business of being a baby, no simple matter in Wolfe's scheme of things. It is in fact a supreme indignity: swarms of adult giants leaning over him, poking, pinching, nudging, making strange mewing sounds, and speaking in that puerile gibberish grown-ups feel compelled to assume when addressing infants. Eugene is a baby straight out of Wordsworth, with a special wisdom of his own. Here he is climbing out of his crib and coming upon his older brother's alphabet blocks:

> Holding them clumsily in his tiny hands, he studied for hours the symbols of speech, knowing that he had here the stones of the temple of language, and striving desperately to find the key that would draw order and intelligence from this anarchy. Great voices soared far above him, vast shapes came and went, lifting him to dizzy heights, depositing him with exhaustless strength. The bell rang under the sea.

What takes the rest of us at least six years to get even an inkling of and then after a struggle, this tot gets at six months, and all at once, in a single intuitive flash. This may be nonsense but—let us rush to say—wonderful nonsense. The stones of the temple of language, great voices soaring above, bells ringing under the sea—the whole universe of air, earth, and water is set vibrating in cosmic unison. We may not believe a word of it. The assault on credibility is certainly total. Yet being put in touch imaginatively with something

larger than ourselves—a typical Wolfe enterprise—is tremendously stirring. It is not only worth the price in terms of
rudely shattered realism but may be achievable only by
paying that price. Wolfe's instinct for the sublime, one of his
priceless assets, does not come cheap. But it comes.

Having had his first climactic experience indoors, Eugene
is ready for his first one outdoors. Spring has come, and with
it one of Wolfe's flowering landscapes:

> When the spongy black earth of the yard was covered
> with sudden, tender grass, and wet blossoms, the great
> cherry tree seethed slowly with a massive gem of amber
> sap, and the cherries hung ripening in prodigal clusters,
> Gant took him from his basket in the sun on the high
> front porch, and went with him around the house by the
> lily beds, taking him back under trees singing with
> hidden birds.

Everything in this landscape is larger than life and larger than
nature: the tree seethes; the sap is massive; the cherry
clusters are prodigal. We are made conscious not only of
spring in the backyard of the Gants, but of spring everywhere, bursting tumultuously all over the earth.

There follow, with the rapid succession of growth itself, a
whole series of sensations and events punctuating the memory of Eugene's early years: Eugene, as a toddler, crawling
onto the road and being trampled on by a horse; Luke
coming down with typhoid; Steve, the oldest son, going
downhill in a series of sullen misadventures; the father
stamping off and getting drunk for days at a time; seam-burst-
ing meals rising to the caloric orgy of Christmas dinner; his
mother saving "bits of old string, empty cans and bottles,
paper, trash of every description"; one sister playing the
piano, the other singing for hours on end; noise, din,

quarreling, voices raised in anger, stretches of drowsy silence—the whole stream of passionate domestic life careening along in a volatile, endless burble. With everything climaxed by food, in mind-boggling quantities. The Gants, trenchermen to the last one, must have set records for ingestion in Old Catawba. Here is a typical day's menu:

> In the morning . . . they sat at a smoking table loaded with brains and eggs, ham, hot biscuit, fried apples seething in their gummed syrups, honey, golden butter, fried steak, scalding coffee. Or there were stacked batter-cakes, rum-colored molasses, fragrant brown sausages, a bowl of wet cherries, plums, fat juicy bacon, jam. At the mid-day meal, they ate heavily: a huge hot roast of beef, fat buttered lima-beans, tender corn smoking on the cob, thick red slabs of sliced tomatoes, rough savory spinach, hot yellow corn-bread, flaky biscuits, a deep-dish peach and apple cobbler spiced with cinnamon, tender cabbage, deep glass dishes piled with preserved fruits—cherries, pears, peaches. At night they might eat fried steak, hot squares of grits fried in egg and butter, pork-chops, fish, young fried chicken.

There is more in this than a savory catalogue of dishes or the rendering of a family with gluttonous appetites. Wolfe is a great epic poet of food, an American Franz Hals. And it is not just the food that he celebrates but the intoxicating joy of eating—an emotion that reaches beyond the salivary glands and the digestive tract to touch some primal instinct of gratification in the flesh. The sense explosion that it registers stretches to the verbal limit the sinews of the language seeking to contain it. Wolfe's habit is to crowd into his words as much energy as they can hold and thus drive them to the bursting point. He is more than a user or even an exploiter of language. He is a tyrant over it.

Orgies of food among the Gants are interspersed with orgies of travel. The act of travel, like the rapture of eating, is another of those essential human experiences Wolfe ecstasizes over and invests with consummate lyric force. Both father and mother have a passion for journeying, but along different orbits. Eliza Gant is fired up by real-estate fever: her aim is to go from one place to another, with the fixed hope of buying land. In 1904 she makes the incredible effort of moving to St. Louis with most of her children, renting and operating a boardinghouse, and settling down to enjoy the World's Fair, not for its own sake, but as a magnet attracting vast sums of money. As it happens, Grover catches typhoid at the Fair and dies, and they all trail home in sorrow, with Eliza wounded almost beyond repair. But the expedition to St. Louis was wholly characteristic of her interest in exploring the world beyond her native mountains. Her objective was immediate and practical, having nothing to do with the usual pleasures of travel.

By contrast, Oliver's traveling is almost disembodied. He journeys for its own sake, as the mood seizes him, and generally to distant parts. After his family returns from St. Louis, he takes off, alone, for California. He has no particular business there, no scheme in mind, no itinerary or schedule drawn up. He simply wanders. In a stylish epithet reminiscent of *Beowulf*, Wolfe calls him "Gant the Far-Wanderer." He leaves for an indeterminate time and returns without advance notice. Neither husband nor wife accompanies the other on these travels, dramatizing the unencompassable distance between them. As the author remarks, she wants to own the earth, he to explore it. Eugene does not go with his father, but we are nonetheless treated to a highly energized, thrillingly picturesque panorama of the American West.

There is the great desert and the vast, alluvial Colorado River winding its way along immense distances. At the ports of Los Angeles and San Francisco ships from the far reaches of the earth, their holds teeming with the odors of rum, tar, molasses, pineapple, cluster as far as the eye can see. Gant brings all these back with him and more: the glamorous names of Louisiana, Texas, Arizona, California; the great canyons and endless mountain ranges; and the vast iridescent western sky, epically beyond the reach of man.

A man who brings all that back with him cannot be allowed to slip unnoticed into town. His return must be announced with fanfare. In Chapter 7, the first of the Joycean chapters in the novel, Wolfe provides him with a homecoming reception in the style of *Ulysses*. The fragmentary instantaneous thoughts, the chopped-up impressions, the bits and pieces bobbing along on the stream of consciousness that mark the mental processes of Leopold Bloom as he wanders through Dublin, reappear in Oliver Gant as he comes back to Altamont. Wolfe is an excellent mimic, and his imitation of Joyce is splendid.

Yet the imitation is inappropriate to the occasion and out of joint. Gant is not Bloom, and forcing him into the rhetorical mold of a man so different from himself damages him badly. Bloom is amiable and mature; Gant, hot-tempered and childish. Bloom's thoughts, often half-baked, are nevertheless rich and varied, and very well suited to interior monologue. Gant's mental life is almost nil; he lives not in concrete ideas but in vague fantasies; he functions in the senses. There are not enough thoughts, ideas, reflections, in him to nourish the interior monologue where, after all, the sentient and producing mind is the sole agent and actor. The result is that the elaborate Joycean technique leaves Gant blank. Thrust into the wrong element, he is left gasping for air. Oliver Gant is one of Wolfe's great creations, but forcing him through the blender of James Joyce was one of Wolfe's major errors in judgment.

As Eugene grows older, he begins to share his creator's penchant for the outsized. When it rains, it is not just ordinary everyday rain that falls; it is "millionfooted rain." Eugene watches his father inscribing tombstones and thinks that his father's work will last forever while the work of grocers, brewers, plumbers is doomed to disappear. The idea of lasting forever takes hold of him early, and feeds his obsession with immortality. He too is destined to be a wordsmith, like his father, but on paper rather than rock, and will one day yearn to write books that will endure as long as his father's stones, enchanting the living and not just commemorating the dead.

As a boy he already prepares for this by indulging in rich, Walter Mitty-like daydreams of heroism, reworking in his mind the plots of popular fiction and romances. Wolfe cannot quite make up his mind whether to treat Eugene's growing-up realistically—describing Eugene and his schoolmates as they play baseball, chew the fat, bait and torment Jews and Negroes—or mythologically, as a young god loitering on the way to school hearing "the reed, the oaten-stop, the running goathoofs in the spongy wood." He throws in both approaches. Eugene is at once a typical little Southern bigot and the great god Pan. These bewildering polarities may not mingle comfortably in the reading, but they suit the author's ultimate purpose as a "putter-inner"; when in doubt, include it all.

In the background, as a perpetual grace note, is brother Ben, affectionate, sardonic, quietly aware of his family's vulgarity and rampant egotism. His is one of the great faces in Wolfe:

> He had aqueous gray eyes, and a sallow bumpy skin. His head was shapely, the forehead high and bony. His hair was crisp, maple-brown. Below his perpetual scowl, his face was small, converging to a point: his extraordinarily sensitive mouth smiled briefly, flickeringly, inwardly— like a flash of light along a blade.

One of the books's triumphs is Wolfe convincing us that Ben is an original and valuable personality, a really *special* kind of human being, so that even when at the end of the novel he returns after his death as a ghost we are as moved by his presence as when he was alive. He is, in any case, treated with greater and more effective restraint than Eugene.

While still a boy, Eugene is endowed with absurdly inflated qualities and virtues. He is a young god, a natural aristocrat, a "million-noted little instrument"; his perceptions are enormously sensitized; he is savagely honest and infinitely superior to the world into which he was born. All this puffery is a drag on the narrative, a thickening layer of psychological fat that interferes with our sympathies. Eugene does not earn or demonstrate these qualities, at least not on the level of exalted superlative. Wolfe simply grade-labels him that way, and he pants and thrashes about throughout the novel under the strain of trying to live up to his billing.

A typical scene: "He rushed at the wall like an insane little goat, battered his head screaming again and again, wished desperately that his constricted and overloaded heart would burst, that something in him would break, that somehow, bloodily, he might escape the stifling prisonhouse of his life." The frenzy and rant in Eugene is a perfectly authentic human trait. Yet Wolfe insists on displaying it not as a characteristic but as a virtue, as a sign of his hero's superiority. On these terms even a charitable reader will find him hard to swallow.

Among his brothers and sisters it is not only Ben who is treated more credibly. So is Helen. Here is a brief but acutely penetrating comment about her: "It was a spiritual and physical necessity for her to exhaust herself in service for others, and it was necessary for her to receive heavy slatherings of praise for that service, and especially necessary that she feel her efforts had gone unappreciated." Unlike Eugene's, her face is recognizably human. Wolfe is not content with giving Eugene anything so ordinary: his face is "remote" and "fabulous." If the reader has trouble figuring out what these adjectives mean in terms of Eugene's face, he will have even greater difficulty with the catch phrase describing his bloodstream: "the Dark Helen burning in Eugene's blood." These words, frequently repeated, sound good; they have a splendid romantic resonance. But what in heaven's name do they mean? It is doubtful that even Wolfe knew. His mythological tendency often ran away with him.

Until he was four, Eugene nursed at his mother's breast, and for years thereafter he continued to sleep in her bed. She fiercely possessed him and hated to let him go. When she opened her boardinghouse—Spend Your Summers at Dixieland in Beautiful Altamont, America's Switzerland, Eliza E. Gant Prop.—Eugene went with her, leaving his father's house and plunging into this new "bleak horror" of a world of transient strangers with whom, nevertheless, one lived, ate, talked, moved about at close quarters and in peculiar intimacy. At the table he listened to "the braided clamor of their talk," one of the novel's most felicitous and expressive phrases. The boarders, chiefly female, fed his instinctive attraction to older women, fixed to start with by his mother's overwhelming closeness.

She took him everywhere on her restless journeys to other places, haggling, bargaining, and scrounging as she went. They traveled all over the South: to Hot Springs, Arkansas, to New Orleans for Mardi Gras, up and down Florida, her eyes avidly alert for profitable real estate. By the end of Part One of the novel, when he is almost twelve, Eugene has already developed strong feelings of aversion and hatred for the South.

He is repelled by the sentimental myths about the South. He did not believe that slavery was a system really good for the slaves, that plantation life was all magnolia and roses, that the Confederate soldiers were always brave and Southern women always beautiful. Even Southern manners, famous the world over, and the Southern accent grated on him. The whole legend of the South, created and nurtured by Southerners to get them through their troubles, seemed to him superstitious and false.

But however much his mind may have rejected the South, his feelings were so intimately bound up with his native region that he could not give them up. He thought about the South incessantly and returned to it perpetually. His attitude, after leaving, was not unlike Joyce's to Ireland: he could not go on living there, yet his imagination could not let it go. Moving over the face of the South while still a small boy firmly attached to his mother's side, Eugene, like Wolfe before him, arrived at an emotional standoff with the place of his origin that was to endure unchanged through "the cool slow passage of the world."

Eugene is now twelve. He becomes conscious of time and longs for it to stand still, a longing tied to his hunger for immortality. With the clock moving, everything changes; mortality triumphs. He clings to the mountains surrounding Altamont: "They were . . . beyond growth, beyond struggle and death. They were his absolute unity in the midst of eternal change." Hearing "the ghostly ticking of his life," he tried to recall the past, for by recalling it he may cause it to freeze forever. "His life coiled back into the brown murk of the past like a twined filament of electric wire," and everything that he could remember he held in the center of his mind for as long as he could.

> There was one moment of timeless suspension when the land did not move, the train did not move, the slattern in the doorway did not move, he did not move. It was as if God had lifted his baton sharply above the endless orchestration of the seas, and the eternal movement had stopped, suspended in the timeless architecture of the absolute. Or like those motion-pictures that describe the movements of a swimmer making a dive, or a horse taking a hedge—movement is petrified suddenly in mid-air, the inexorable completion of an act is arrested.

Wolfe had read Keats and absorbed the terrific moment in "To Autumn," the last of Keats's great odes, when the old man with the scythe goes to sleep briefly at harvest time, all of nature suspends its operations, and the whole universe— time, space, everything—escapes the remorseless process of movement and change for one breathtaking instant. At various times the other figures in the novel are seen in the same light. Each one freezes into an image of his earlier being as though gazing at a younger replica of himself in some photograph taken years before. The previous likeness seems for the moment more real than the present reality. This exchange of identity is accompanied by a remarkable suspension of the physical universe. Even the water in the fountain of the town square is arrested in midair, the spray floating motionless against the circumambient sky.

As time unfreezes and motion resumes its course, the three directions of the novel become intensely visible: Eugene going up; his father, now in the early stages of his fatal illness, going down; his mother tenaciously creeping along on her horizontal track. Each of these directions is embodied in a significant episode, climaxing Part Two of the novel. With Eugene, it is his entry into Mr. Leonard's school. There he comes under the sway of Mrs. Leonard, one of those remarkable teachers who actually do inspire the young. With her as a guide, he is made aware of the glories of English literature and is excited by the attractions of the intellectual life.

Typical of this stretch of experience is Chapter 24, another of the Joycean chapters but this time perfectly suited to its subject: complete with stream-of-consciousness outbursts which Eugene's overheated and excitable mind, as well as those of his schoolmates, have no trouble filling. And the splicing of lines from the great English poets is worthy of the model it imitates: Joyce's extraordinary re-creation of the great styles in English literature during the Oxen of the Sun chapter in *Ulysses*.

Oliver Gant's downward turn is symbolized by his sale of the angel. He had acquired it years before, and it had become the unattainable life ideal he could not hope to reproduce.

> It was now brown and fly-specked. But it had come from Carrara in Italy, and it held a stone lily delicately in one hand. The other hand was lifted in benediction, it

was poised clumsily upon the ball of one phthisic foot,
and its stupid white face wore a smile of soft stone
idiocy.

Its idiotic smile, its phthisic foot, its clumsy stance, its
flyspecked appearance, all suggest Gant's failure in the
world, the second-rate nature of his life: his failure as an
artist, as a husband, his failure to harness his own superb
vitality. Now he sells the angel to the town madam, an act
that leaves "a barren crater in his heart." One of her girls has
died, and she has come to select a tombstone. Something
sentimental in the aspect of the angel appeals to her, and she
orders it, with an appropriately sugary eight lines of verse
that Gant will chisel on the stone.

The whole scene, with its rueful commentary on Gant, is
faultlessly rendered and ends on an appropriate note of
pathos. As he escorts her out of his shop, they look at each
other, remembering—with sadness and pleasure—the passage of professional love between them long before. The
recalled emotion is genuine, considerably purified by the
passage of time, yet the element of tenderness in it is in
poignant contrast to his relationship, not professional at all
but sanctified by marriage, with Eliza. There had been much
early passion in their marriage, followed by a seemingly
endless skein of frustration, disappointment, denial, bitter-
ness, and hatred. In this whole seamy catalogue, there was no
tenderness. He was to find that only in the arms of a whore.

Eliza's profoundest association in the novel is not with her
husband or children but with her boardinghouse, Dixieland.
Dixieland is only around the corner from the house where her
married life had begun and her children born, but when she
moves to it the break with her marriage ties is final. Oliver
visits, rants, entertains the boarders, eats and sleeps there

occasionally, falls ill and is nursed there, but he is not in residence. The essential characteristic of Dixieland, where Eliza is the proprietor, the creator and reigning spirit, is its sameness. The guests come and go with the seasons. The children are sent to meet the incoming trains with advertising cards at exactly the same time each year. The meals, the romances, the throbbing transience of boardinghouse routine, repeat themselves with inflexible regularity.

All this perfectly expresses and richly satisfies the soul of Eliza Gant. She owns Dixieland, controls its operations, speculates pleasurably on how it might rise in value, and in the off-season goes to other cities with other seasons and runs boardinghouses there. She is a dedicated professional, just as her husband is an irrepressible amateur. The professional, by mastering the circumstances of his trade, imposes his devotion and skill upon the hazards of time and change.

Eliza seems to go on and on, indefatigable, unconquerable. She suffers terrible misfortunes and is deeply wounded—by the death of Grover; the parting with Oliver; the inevitable separation from Eugene, "the last coinage of her flesh," to whom she maternally clings with a kind of atavistic ferocity; the later collapse of the real-estate boom in Altamont which all but ruins her. Her ultimate self remains undamaged and intact. After each disaster, she resumes her slow, onward pace on the same track as before. She embodies the principle of changelessness, a principle as deeply embedded in nature and in life as the principle of flux embodied in her husband and sons.

The third and final section of the novel is devoted largely to Eugene's four years at the state university. After all the works of fiction devoted to the education of young men, it is difficult even for Wolfe to say anything very new about it, and he does not. Eugene in college goes through the standard procedures. As a freshman he is ragged and bullied because he is abnormally thin, tall, and gawky. He is initiated into sex by knowing classmates who lead him to neighboring brothels. He is stimulated by an occasional instructor, falls in love with the eighteenth-century writers and is put off by the Victorian ones, forms friendships, gets into mild scrapes, lets off steam, is rebellious and iconoclastic, writes, goes out for the college newspaper and literary magazine, longs to join the war in Europe which America has now entered, and is acutely disappointed when he is too young to enlist.

We are treated to a full catalogue of his thoughts on these matters, most of them sophomoric and virtually all of them familiar. He begins to seem like everyone else, even to himself. "What, he thought, can I be, besides a genius? I've been one long enough. There must be better things to do." He makes mild efforts to discover what some of these better things are. When he doesn't succeed, he goes back to being a genius. That is, of course, what he secretly wants to be. It is his natural vocation. And in the end he proves to be good at it.

Liberal applications of humor by Wolfe make this vocation bearable. After a particularly florid burst of self-praise, Eugene is so overcome with emotion he is forced to blow his nose. Later, he spins out fantasies of playing the hero in the war. He and the dean of the college exchange clichés on the subject: Eugene proposes to defend his mother and sister from the murderous Huns who raped Little Belgium. The dean observes solemnly that the "Future of Mankind hangs in the balance." Thus pumping them up into a mutual ecstasy, Wolfe thrusts home his comic needle in a Joycean phrase:

"Deeply stirred they stood together for a moment, drenched in the radiant beauty of their heroic souls."

Eugene's eagerness to enlist is treated broadly: "By Spring, if God was good, all the proud privileges of trench-lice, mustard gas, spattered brains, punctured lungs, ripped guts, asphyxiation, mud and gangrene, might be his. . . . He saw himself as Ace Gant, the falcon of the skies, with 63 Huns to his credit by his nineteenth year. He saw himself walking up the Champs-Elysées, with a handsome powdering of gray hair above his temples, a left forearm of the finest cork, and the luscious young widow of a French marshal at his side. For the first time he saw the romantic charm of mutilation."

When Eugene is feeling paranoid—the idea that the world is ranged in an immense conspiracy against him is one of his favorite and most comforting notions—he dreams of himself as the great man playing all the leading roles in history: President Gant, Jesus-of-Nazareth Gant, François-Villon Gant, Edward-the-Black-Prince Gant, Vercingetorix Gant, Ivan-the-Terrible Gant, and so on. The last name on the list, however, the one that deflates the rest, is Mumbo-Jumbo Gant.

Sometimes the humor is arch. Playing his little game of registering at different hotels under the names of celebrated English writers, Eugene comes to a hotel in a small Piedmont town where he signs in as Ben Jonson.

> The clerk spun the book critically.
> "Isn't there an *h* in that name?" he said.
> "No," said Eugene. "That's another branch of the family. I have an uncle, Samuel, who spells his name that way."

Arch or not, the touch of lighthearted fun is welcome. It

leavens and cools the boiling landscape of Eugene's autoin-
toxicated self.

Wolfe's diction careens wildly and uncertainly between
the trite and the obscure. He will sink into banalities: "Her
touch shot through him like a train of fire." "She throbbed in
the beat of his pulses. She was wine in his blood, a music in
his heart." "A great light wind swept over the water . . .
making a music and a glory in his heart." He is given to the
elocutionist exclamations of the nineteenth century: O God!
O lost! O my young love! O sea! But he will then veer off to
the other extreme and come up with rare, strange, at times
quite wonderful, words and sentences. He uses words like
stogged, helve, glozed, adyt, weft, ensymplastic, encysted,
agglutinated, marly, moil, stype, thrum, chrysm, reluctation.

Some of his sentences are dazzling. Here is one, among the
finest in *Look Homeward, Angel*: "Fluescent with smooth
ripe curves, the drawling virgins of the South filled summer
porches." Or: "The blue gulf of the sky was spread with light
massy clouds: they cruised like swift galleons, tacking across
the hills before the wind, and darkening the trees below with
their floating shadows." Or "the vast moon-meadows of the
night" as an example of his gift for eloquent epithets. He is
the great purveyor of the rhetorical smorgasbord, with
something in it for every taste, vulgar and exquisite alike. The
brilliant spectrum of his language alone instantly refutes the
widespread feeling that he is a one-note, one-key writer.

Eugene's life continues off-campus as well as on. One
summer he falls in love with a young woman some years older
than himself boarding at Dixieland. He is in love half with
her, half with the emotion she arouses in him. He milks his
feelings at both ends: the joy of attraction to a responsive

human being, the deeply pleasurable pathos of frustration when she turns out to be engaged to someone else and the episode comes to a painful end.

At home, too, the family tragedy continues to unwind. The father, in the grip of his terrible disease, has grown wasted and thin: "The cancer, Eugene thought, flowered in him like some terrible but beautiful plant." But he refuses to die. "He hung to life by a decayed filament, a corpse lit by infrequent flares of consciousness." He survives long enough to endure again one of the great shocks of parenthood, another of his children dying before him. Ben this time, felled by the flu epidemic at the end of the war, following his twin Grover into premature death. Ben retains his bitter intelligence to the last, the final moment given a transcendence that is profoundly, exaltedly moving.

> But suddenly, marvellously, as if his resurrection and rebirth had come upon him, Ben drew upon the air in a long and powerful respiration; his gray eyes opened. Filled with a terrible vision of all life in the one moment, he seemed to rise forward bodilessly from his pillows without support . . . and, casting the fierce sword of his glance with utter and final comprehension upon the room haunted with its gray pageantry of cheap loves and dull consciences and on all those uncertain mummers of waste and confusion fading now from the bright window of his eyes, he passed instantly, scornful and unafraid, as he had lived, into the shades of death.

Eugene graduates from college and prepares to leave for the North. Before that, however, comes his angry, bitterly sarcastic repudiation of his family:

> I give thanks for the country slut who nursed me and let my dirty bandage fester across my navel. I give thanks

for every blow and curse I had from any of you during
my childhood, for every dirty cell you ever gave me to
sleep in, for the ten million hours of cruelty or
indifference, and the thirty minutes of cheap advice.
. . . By God, I shall spend the rest of my life getting my
heart back, healing and forgetting every scar you put
upon me when I was a child. The first move I ever
made, after the cradle, was to crawl for the door, and
every move I have made since has been an effort to
escape.

But he also sees them as epic figures. He compares his
father to a fallen Titan, his mother to a blind but powerful
force of earthly accumulation. Helen's life may be futile, her
energies wasted, but there is something awesome about her,
some greatness that commands our admiration. And Ben
carries out his role as ghost and stranger in this world with
absolute, unflinching finality.

These conflicting views, far from paralyzing him, trigger a
series of ecstatic responses which, rising in intensity, bring
the novel to an end. There is his paean to drink, running up
to peaks of manic enthusiasm. After paying tribute to the
power and glory of liquor, he exults over the length of his
arms, legs, and body; there is that much more of him to be
filled by the fruits of the grape. Since it is possible for him to
feel like a god when drunk, he longs to be drunk forever.

A frenzied life-intoxication seizes him. He feels ecstasy
pouring through his limbs, extracting from him frenzied
screams of joy, and sending him careening through the
countryside like an unguided missile. If only he could lay
hands on, if only he could control this tremendous ferment
inside him, he might even become immortal. He grows
delirious about his own body, which he regards as more
sublime than all other bodies on earth: "The web of my flesh

is finer; my blood is a subtle elixir: the hair of my head, the marrow of my spine, the cunning jointure of my bones, and all the combining jellies, fats, meats, oils, and sinews of my flesh, the spittle of my mouth, the sweat of my skin, is mixed with rarer elements, and is fairer and finer than their gross peasant beef."

Thus racing along, with squeals and wild goatlike cries pouring from his throat, he goes forth to conquer and consume the world as though it were an endless banquet of food and drink arranged for him to devour. At increasing speed, the book pounds along to the last episode, Eugene's rendezvous with the ghost of Ben. " 'Where is the world?' " Eugene asks him. Borrowing freely from Milton's Satan and Shakespeare's Hamlet, the ghost replies, " '*You* are your world.' " Eugene needs no further assurance. The reality of his inner self is confirmed by the voice from beyond, ratified by the renewed and thrilling presence of his beloved brother's purified spirit. He leaps to the following resolution: "In the city of myself, upon the continent of my soul, I shall find the forgotten language, the lost world, a door where I may enter."

Turning "his eyes upon the distant soaring ranges" surrounding his native town, he is now poised, in his twentieth year, to take off for the larger world beyond. To this enterprise he brings two special qualities: an omnivorous fascination with everyone and everything, and a relentless memory. His cosmic enthusiasm reaches the force of a passion:

> He was devoured by a vast strange hunger for life. At night he listened to the million-noted ululation of little night things, the great brooding symphony of dark, the ringing of remote churchbells across the country. And

his vision widened out in circles over moon-drenched meadows, dreaming woods, mighty rivers going along in darkness, and ten thousand sleeping towns. He believed in the infinite rich variety of all the towns and faces: behind any of a million shabby houses he believed there was strange buried life, subtle and shattered romance, something dark and unknown.

To Ben's ghost he testifies to the power of his memory: " 'I remember the fly I swallowed on the peach, and the little boys on tricycles at Saint Louis, and the mole on Grover's neck, and the Lackawanna freight-car, number 16356, on a siding near Gulfport. Once, in Norfolk, an Australian soldier on his way to France asked me the way to a ship; I remember that man's face.' "

Leaving Eugene fully grown and well armed for his assault on experience, let us turn briefly to the book that frames him. *Look Homeward, Angel* has all the standard traits of its type, the novel of young growth and education, and the equally established elements of the first novel. It covers the formative years of Eugene's life, dwelling at leisure on parents, teachers, schoolmates, siblings, town, region, and the like. It studies and projects from the moment of birth the young man's feelings, conceptions of himself and others, hopes, dreams, fantasies, passions. Since the baby, then the boy, then the youth, thrashes about unevenly and spontaneously, the shape of the book is sufficiently loose so that the author can stuff into it—as Wolfe generously does—any of his stray thoughts, random reveries, and urgent statements on the Meaning of Things. In this, *Look Homeward, Angel* follows along the well-grooved tracks of its well-known predecessors: *Tom Jones, Wilhelm Meister, David Copperfield, The Ordeal of Richard Feverel, Sons and Lovers,* and *The Portrait of the Artist as a Young Man.* Though generally derivative, it is also specifically imitative, selecting as its model that magnetic pole of modern literature, James Joyce.

It is a first novel as well, with the expected mixture of naïveté and calculation, of surprise and joy, at the very act of self-expression. Its taste and judgments are uncertain but its energy abounding. The writing has extended moments of banality, bathos, and rant, easily equaled, however, by periods of superlative eloquence, interludes of phenomenal virtuosity, and phrasemaking of the highest order. One feels the hovering voice and presence of the novelist throughout, so that he is as vivid a figure in the book as any of his characters. The detachment and perspective, the distancing of the author from his story, that are supposed to come with later novels—qualities that are associated with "maturity" and that are often substitutes for the loss of the original élan—are not yet in evidence.

Look Homeward, Angel differs from the usual promising first novel not by the presence of any original elements as such but in the intensification of the standard elements present in all the others. Multiply the familiar beyond a certain point, and it will cease being familiar; it will seem new. Endowed with abnormal energy and driven by an abnormal longing for success, fame, and immortality, Wolfe drove the "first" novel far beyond its normal limits. When broken down into its component parts, *Look Homeward, Angel* is a perfectly recognizable novel. In the reading, however, it is a novel that is straining to be something else. It is straining to be an epic. Its true originality lies in the fact that it almost succeeds.

And it refutes the pervasive notion that Wolfe is limited to the mind and consciousness of his romantic hero—Eugene Gant here, George Webber later—and can write only from the viewpoint of the adolescent egoist. Eliza and Ben are neither romantic heroes nor adolescent egoists, yet they are more brilliantly drawn and more intimately present in the book than even Eugene. Oliver Gant, the fourth of the dramatically realized figures, is a romantic adolescent of sorts but in a scheme of reference so strikingly different from Eugene's that he is a character wholly separable from his son even while the resemblance between them renders his paternity credible.

There are dozens of lesser personalities in the novel that run up and down the human scale at considerable distances from Eugene's position in it. Over the years readers and critics have been so bemused by Eugene, and by the author whom he so obviously resembles, that they have emerged with a claustrophobic impression of Wolfe's psychological range. *Look Homeward, Angel* teems with evidence to the contrary.

It suggests, indeed, that he had the option of going on from this beginning in almost any direction he chose. It was not just that he had displayed the ability to create a wide variety of characters. He had also supplied examples of various types of fiction. A cursory culling of *Look Homeward, Angel* will reveal the stream-of-consciousness novel in the style of Joyce; the objective-study-of-society novel in the vein of Balzac, Dreiser, and Sinclair Lewis; the apocalyptic-visionary novel of Melville and Dostoevsky; and the novel of argument as practiced by D. H. Lawrence, working its way angrily and feverishly toward a message that will redeem the world. In his first novel Wolfe tried his hand successfully at all these. In the work that followed he was free to pursue any of them.

He chose instead to do something altogether astonishing: to write novels that were not really novels at all, but something profoundly different.

3

Of Time and the River

✥✥ Another of the set judgments about Wolfe that needs correction is that he was doomed by his temperament, by the narrow range of his talent, to write the same book over and over again. But whatever his temperament, his talent was broad enough for him to write a second book that was a striking departure from the first. *Of Time and the River* still has Eugene Gant as its central figure, but there its resemblance to *Look Homeward, Angel* ends.

A key to the difference, and indeed to Wolfe's radical departure from the traditional novel, lay in a statement near the end of *Look Homeward, Angel*. To the author, "the passions of life were greater than the actors." Henceforth he is to deal more and more with the passions, less and less with the actors. The later novels are to be less concerned with the individual characters—even the two heroes will often be seen standing about idly or disappearing altogether while the main business of the books goes on—and more with the painting of impersonal matter: social and geographical landscapes; voyages by train or ship; psychological portraits of the souls not only of men but of cities—New York, London, Munich, Paris; projections of semimythological figures like Bascom Pentland, Dick Prosser, and Nebraska Crane, each of whom possesses some special passion or some particular genius that lifts him beyond the ordinarily human.

The three later novels rapidly shed their novelistic trappings and connections, and assume their real identity. They are not novels but murals, not works of fiction but tableaux. They do not have plots; their story lines are sketchy, tenuous, and erratic; they defy outlining. Unlike the intricately detailed, labyrinthine constructs of Henry James, they can easily be broken up into separate sections. It did not fundamentally matter where Max Perkins ordered *Of Time and the River* brought to a halt or on what basis Edward Aswell hacked out the texts of *The Web and the Rock* and *You Can't Go Home Again* after Wolfe's death. Almost any arrangement would have served since these works do not depend on structural arrangement in usual fictional terms.

Typical of Wolfe's intention to represent rather than fictionalize was his passion to record what was transient and fleeting, what he could not possibly get to know intimately and from the inside. On a fast-moving train passing through a small town, Eugene sees men eating in a diner. He sees them for an instant and will never see them again. Yet he is seized with an urge to describe that one evanescent moment, as somehow representative of what all the eaters in all the diners in the country are doing. He is looking at them not as novelist: a novelist penetrates and individualizes his characters. He is looking at them as a painter or sculptor, seeing in their posture something revealing and essential. This is a tableau, a detail for his endlessly expanding mural not so much about men and women and the story of their lives as about the nature, texture, and "feel" of experience. His impulse was to go beyond the unique and particular, and seize the representational, which was another way of allying himself with the permanent.

There are Parisian street scenes painted by Utrillo that illustrate Wolfe's direction. Utrillo does have persons spotted here and there, but their faces are seldom visible. They are recognizably men or women; they carry umbrellas on rainy days; they walk, stand still, have distinctive postures, but they remain impersonalized and abstract, human figures rather than human beings, and in any case only one among a number of equally important elements. The cobblestones glistening in the rain are just as important; so are the narrow sidewalks, the walls of the houses lining the streets, the irregular segments of sky, and the pervasive light shifting from gray to green to golden. The elements contribute to the scene, but it is the scene as a whole that stands out and mutes the particularities.

Look Homeward, Angel focused on Eugene. It wandered off at times to other matters—Ben in his newspaper office, conversations in bars, sketches of town life in none of which Eugene appeared—but it always came back to him. In *Of Time and the River* there is a persistent undertow *away* from him. The process goes on intermittently through the novel and is never completed. But the best things in it are the scenes where Eugene is only a bystander or at most a convenient observing eye; indeed, the most tiresome and prolix sections are those that center around his private self.

Wolfe himself was conscious of this process in his second

novel, and even said that he was fed up with Eugene and with Eugene Gant-ness. For his third and fourth books he created a new protagonist, George Webber, who is much less the center of attention than Eugene, while the drift away from traditional storytelling, away from the actors and toward the passions of life continues with ever-accelerating speed. It ends up with the paradox that Wolfe, generally thought of as the most personal of all writers, should strive in his later art for the ultimately impersonal, moving away from the ego of the individual to the face of the universe.

The books he planned to write, far more numerous than the ones he actually did, illustrate this movement even more clearly. One was to be "my book of the night," about America at night and "how the Americans are a night-time people." He describes it in a letter to Perkins:

> I don't know yet exactly what form it will take, or whether it can be called a "novel" or not. I don't care—but I think it will be a great tone-symphony of night-railway yards, engines, freights, dynamos, bridges, men and women, the wilderness, plains rivers, deserts, a clopping hoof, etc.—seen *not by a definite personality*, but haunted throughout by a consciousness of *personality*. In other words, I want to assert my divine right once and for all to be the *God Almighty* of a book—
> . . . to blast forever the charge of "autobiography" while being triumphantly and impersonally autobiographical.

It is not a novel he is after but a tone symphony. Men and women are no less important but no more so than engines, bridges, deserts, rivers. And the definite personality—i.e., the traditional hero, or antihero—is to be replaced by the omniscient author playing the role of an impersonal God.

So while it has been part of conventional opinion to regard Wolfe as a latter-day romantic with his roots in Wordsworth, Shelley, and Keats, he traveled a great distance from these beginnings and wound up among the postwar expressionists. If *Look Homeward, Angel* exploits Wordsworth's worship of the preternaturally wise and intuitive child, and Keats's passion for fame and immortality, the later novels resemble just as closely the expressionist plays of Frank Wedekind, Stefan George, Ernst Toller, and Elmer Rice, and even more closely the new expressionist fictions of John Dos Passos.

Manhattan Transfer and *The 42nd Parallel*, two of Dos Passos's early novels written in the twenties, displace the individual character in favor of extrafictional techniques borrowed from the movies, newspapers, engineering, biography, history, art, and the fresh forms being thrown up by industrial technology. Among the modern Americans, Dos Passos is the guerrilla raider of letters, as Joyce is among the Europeans, invading, stealing, and importing into fiction devices and ideas from other genres. Joyce's favorite nonfictional device was the stream-of-consciousness monologue, which he adapted from psychoanalysis. Dos Passos plays on a whole repertory of new modes: camera eyes, newsreels, incantatory prose poems borrowed from the Psalms and the Prophets, portraits of actual historical figures heightened and energized so that they seem fictional. Forcing history to imitate art was one of his supreme objectives.

What he was really after was not people or the study of human nature, but the reading of civilization—an immense, impersonal, and quite abstract aim. He began modestly enough in *Manhattan Transfer* with a recapitulation of New York City. In *The 42nd Parallel* and its two companion novels, *1919* and *The Big Money*, he adventurously expanded this aim to cover nothing less than American civilization itself during the first thirty years of the twentieth century. He floated a number of fictional characters in his historical-fictional grab bag, but they were only one of several tools designed to seize his larger subject, and his interest in them was purely instrumental: they do not exist in these books as ends in themselves, as they do in the novels of Dickens and George Eliot; they are servants of a larger purpose, in this instance the face and soul of a nation. In his later work Dos Passos abandoned these expressionist procedures and principles—which he had carried out with so much dash—and went back to the writing of conventional novels. This depressed both his art and his reputation.

Wolfe's analogous pursuit of absolutes, his disengagement from conventional fiction began with *Of Time and the River*, and continued without letup to the end of his career. The fourth and last published novel, *You Can't Go Home Again*, is much more an assemblage of set pieces, loosely tied together with fictional filaments, than is the second. The established judgment with regard to Wolfe is that his finest, most successfully realized novel is *Look Homeward, Angel*, after which there is a marked falling off. If the four are to be regarded as standard novels, the judgment is not to be seriously quarreled with.

If, however, the last three, which is to say the bulk of his work, are to be regarded not as novels in the familiar sense° but as something else, something altogether different, even radically different, then the established judgment collapses. It is my argument that they should be so regarded, indeed that

---

° Edward Aswell recalled that Wolfe seldom referred to his works as novels but simply as books. He referred to himself as an author or writer, never as a novelist.

in terms of their demonstrable character and structure they compel us to. In that case the wrong criteria have been applied, and Wolfe has been read in the wrong focus. Any serious revaluation of his ultimate achievement must begin at this point.

His notorious and well-publicized difficulties in finishing *Of Time and the River* can now be explained in another way. He had trouble finishing because, in fact, he was writing something that was not "finishable." Straight novels, whether written by Defoe and Fielding in the eighteenth century or by Saul Bellow and Iris Murdoch in the twentieth, *are* finishable: they are maneuvered by their internal form to have a beginning, middle, and end of some sort, however rough and informal.

In this respect Aristotle himself could have found little fault with *Look Homeward, Angel.* Its three stages are self-evident: beginning (Eugene's birth), middle (his growing-up), end (on the verge of leaving home and setting off on his own). *Of Time and the River* begins with Eugene on a train platform, waiting to leave Altamont. This is a recognizable and authentic beginning, but there the expected sequence ends. With the start of the train journey carrying Eugene North, the book lurches away from its tie with *Look Homeward, Angel* and goes off on a direction of its own.

From this moment forward, it steadily loses its capacity to be finished. Perkins's arbitrary decision to end it at a certain point was not an aesthetic judgment but a commercial one. As the publisher, he wanted to bring out a second book by Wolfe before the success of the first had utterly faded from view. The ending he decided on—Eugene's meeting Mrs. Jack aboard ship—is not satisfactory if the book is considered as a traditional novel; it abruptly introduces a new character and a new relationship, so that the end is not really the end but a new beginning. Almost six years after the appearance of *Look Homeward, Angel*, confronted with an author who moaned aloud at the thought of finishing and pleaded on every occasion for just six months more, Perkins was driven to extreme measures.

What Perkins did not realize, what Wolfe himself was only vaguely conscious of at this time, was that he had slipped into a literary mode from which the orthodox milestones and landmarks had vanished, a mode based on scene, passage, and bas-relief rather than on character, story, and sequence. Where the book ended did not really matter; one place was as good—or as bad—as another. In the complex misunderstandings and tensions of 1934–35, Wolfe suffered a special kind of authorial misery, and there sprang up between him and Perkins a sore point that was never to be resolved.

The attacks by the critics on Wolfe's books from here on, beginning with Bernard De Voto's savage assault on *Of Time and the River*, are based on a fundamental misconception of their real nature. To complain about their rambling structures, excess verbiage, emotional overheatedness, loose ends, with the author going off with mad irrelevance in all directions would be perfectly valid were they normal novels, or even abnormal ones. Since they are not, these criticisms are themselves largely irrelevant. The fact that Wolfe himself accepted the premises on which they were based and suffered so mordantly from them, the fact that he was only dimly aware of the altering shape of his own art, make them no less so.

At the start of the book itself, the reader must again thread his way through a thicket of preliminaries. There is the cosmic subtitle: *A Legend of Man's Hunger in His Youth*, suggesting Wolfe's movement from men to Man, from the individual to the species. Still on the title page, a quotation from the Bible appears, referring to the spirit of man and beast, archetypal figures on a canvas larger than life.

Then comes the dedication to Perkins. Wolfe was given to fervid and admiring dedications, and this is one of them, full of praise and gratitude. Wolfe even manages to deliver himself over to enemies like De Voto by asserting that his book could not have been written without his editor's care and devotion. A passage from Plato about listening to unearthly voices, a table of contents in which each of the novel's eight books is given a mythological tag, three stanzas in German from a romantic poem by Goethe describing an ideal country, and an outburst of italicized purple prose on the subject of loneliness and death bring us at last to page one—where Eugene, in 1920, is on the Altamont train platform, accompanied by his mother, his sister Helen and her husband, waiting for the train that will take him away from the South, his mother's country, to the North, his father's.

A number of pages are consumed in expressive chatter, the characters revealing themselves and their mutual feelings as they had in the first novel. At last the train arrives, and with it *Of Time and the River* starts off on its own. The train is, of course, no ordinary train, but a demonic apparition from some other kingdom that Wolfe conjures up with help from Dante. With its huge black snout

> The locomotive . . . loomed enormously above them
> . . . with a terrific drive of eight-locked pistoned wheels
> . . . a savage furnace-flair of heat, a hard hose-thick hiss

of steam, a huge tangle of gauges, levers, valves, and throttles, and the goggled blackened face of the fireman, lit by an intermittent hell of flame. . . .

The locomotive passed above them, darkening the sunlight from their faces . . . drawing the souls out through their mouths with the God-head of its instant absoluteness.

The fifty-page train journey that follows lives up to this advance billing. It is a brilliant demonstration of the new Wolfe, and the first large-scale example of where he is heading. What he sees from the window of the speeding train or from depot platforms during stops is registered not through a novelist's eye but a muralist's.

Towns, streets, squares bathed in limpid moonlight, movie houses briefly glimpsed, cabins teetering perilously on the side of hills, women standing in front of them with snuff sticks in their mouths and ragged urchins in their arms, the dazzling alternation of landscape between towering peaks and sudden flat plains—these do not feed the understanding or exposition of the characters observing them but are ends in themselves. Eugene is there to serve *them;* they are not there to serve him. He talks with people on the train; he visits his dying father in a Baltimore hospital. These moments are not used to advance our knowledge of Eugene. He does not grow or change, is not revealed during their course. They are interludes, breathing spells, while author and reader gather themselves for the next phase of the journey.

Much of it takes place in darkness, and Wolfe is extraordinary at seizing the phantasmal shapes and depths of night. He speaks of the past as "lost at the bottom of the million-visaged sea-depth of dark time." He rings every variation on the nocturnal theme, playing over the range of darkness like an impassioned xylophonist: the velvet-breasted night, the black dark of a winter's morning, Eugene flinging papers "against the shack-walls of the jungle-sleeping blacks" in Niggertown, the great trains of America hurtling on "through darkness over the lonely, everlasting earth," "the million-footed ululation of the night," and dozens of other ecstatic verbal outbursts on night landscape. They all come to a climax in this celebrated lunar passage:

> Then the moon blazed down upon the vast desolation of the American coasts, and on all the glut and hiss of tides, on all the surge and foaming slide of waters on lone beaches. The moon blazed down on 18,000 miles of coast, on the million sucks and scoops and hollows of the shore, and on the great wink of the sea, that ate the earth minutely and eternally. The moon blazed down upon the wilderness, it fell on sleeping woods, it dripped through moving leaves, it swarmed in weaving patterns on the earth, and it filled the cat's still eye with blazing yellow. The moon slept over mountains and lay like silence in the desert, and it carved the shadows of great rocks like time. The moon was mixed with flowing rivers, and it was buried in the heart of lakes, and it trembled on the water like bright fish. . . .
>
> And in woodland darkness great birds fluttered to their sleep—in sleeping woodlands strange and secret birds, the teal, the nightjar, and the flying rail went to their sleep with flutterings dark as hearts of sleeping men. In fronded beds and on the leaves of unfamiliar plants where the tarantula, the adder, and the asp had fed themselves asleep on their own poisons, and on lush jungle depths where green-golden, bitter red and glossy blue proud tufted birds cried out with brainless scream, the moonlight slept.

Later, as Eugene watches the milling crowds in the Boston railroad station, we come upon the title of the book:

> They streamed in and out of the portals of that
> enormous station in unceasing swarm; great trains
> steamed in to empty them, and others steamed out
> loaded with their nameless motes of lives, and all was
> . . . moving, changing, swarming on forever like a river,
> and as fixed, unutterable in unceasing movement and in
> changeless change as the great river is, and time itself.

Again this moment in the station, like the long train journey that precedes it, suggests the universal rather than the particular: all station scenes in all the stations everywhere in the world are like this one. And again there is no visible effect upon Eugene who is there to record it as Wolfe himself would were it convenient for Wolfe to appear as himself. Eugene is present not as a character in the novel but as the author's willed and obedient surrogate. He records far more than he reacts.

After getting settled at Harvard, Eugene looks up his uncle Bascom Pentland, who had migrated to Boston years before and undergone a startling change of life from preacher to real-estate operator. No fewer than forty-five pages are devoted to Uncle Bascom; and his portrait, on the heels of the train journey, is the second extended section of the Trojan horse Wolfe is building inside the framework of his novel. At first glance this uncle resembles one of Sherwood Anderson's grotesques, a stunted plant in the weedy garden of Winesburg, Ohio. He is stingy, irascible, eccentric, prudish, quarrelsome, and given to loud disputes on all occasions grave or trivial.

But these qualities, which in Anderson are accompanied by handwringing and shrill lamentations of self-pity, here burst forth with deafening exuberance. The world does not press in upon Uncle Bascom; he presses out upon the world and bends it to his stamp. Expression rather than impression is his keynote. Like so many of Wolfe's figures, he does not merely live; he makes expeditionary raids upon life, forcing himself upon the universe. Spread over the Boston landscape, he is a cartoon of gigantic size, each of his lineaments etched in ferocious detail.

If *Of Time and the River* is read as a novel about the further experiences of Eugene Gant, the lengthy appearance of Uncle Bascom can only be taken as a bizarre digression. Though he assaults his nephew with torrential advice on morality, and provides him with priceless entertainment in his legal-theological harangues with motorists, clients, indeed anyone who happens to be around—harangues so intricate, protracted, and noisy as to arouse whole neighborhoods—his effect on Eugene is zero. And if it is Eugene's story we are anxious to get on with, Uncle Bascom's prolonged presence must be regarded as catastrophic to the development of the novel at this point. If, however, we look upon the book as a sequence of sculptures and frescoes, the portrait of Uncle Bascom—it is indeed more than a portrait, it is a vibrant phenomenon—is an absolute marvel of energy and strength. He is one of the great clowns in the pantheon of the grotesque.

That is the end of Uncle Bascom. The book goes on for another seven hundred pages, but he is never heard from or referred to again. There he stands emblazoned on the wall of the novel, autonomous, separable, a huge panel unto himself. Other scenes follow, in the same manner. One is Wolfe's account of the ideal baseball game, with the legendary Christy Mathewson pitching and the legendary Tris Speaker playing center field, and all of America, up to and including Ben Gant, briefly resurrected for the occasion in his newspaper office in Altamont, hanging in exalted and timeless suspense on every move. Again, Eugene is nowhere in sight. The moment-to-moment life of the novel, such as it is, is again obliterated, and we are drawn into an altogether different kind of world, where the absolute and the consummate have replaced immediate reality with all its incompleteness and limitations.

Yet without that reality being securely established, the process cannot work. The key to Wolfe's credibility is his tenacious hold on realistic, even documentary detail. Speaker and Mathewson were legendary ballplayers to be sure, but they were also actual ones. Their actuality, their flesh-and-blood existence, is the indispensable point of departure for the passage to the legendary, toward the moment when they change into the eternal. The baseball game Wolfe describes resembles the real games played on countless occasions everywhere, yet it emerges by itself as the ultimate, the supreme representation of baseball.

The search for the enduring essence of things locked inside their immediate existence is the aim of Wolfe's tableau art. In this he is profoundly different from Plato who also searched for ideal essences but sought to purge them of their ties with the world of sense. Wolfe roots himself in the world of sense. That is his jumping-off place. In his pursuit of the representational, he does not want to leave the sensory behind or get rid of it, but take it with him; it is the ground that feeds, sustains, and makes credible his drive for the ideal. It is because Uncle Bascom exists in the flesh, because the locomotive on the train journey north exists in actuality that Wolfe can release them into the ultimate. The success of his art in its new direction begins with the accuracy and vividness of his sense perceptions.

This is illustrated once again in the next great scene of the book, the death of old Gant. Perhaps the most celebrated account of death in modern literature appears in Tolstoy's "The Death of Ivan Ilyich." There it is all darkness and terror, a suffocating envelope into which the dying man slides by slow degrees. Oliver Gant dies in the opposite manner, in an ecstatic transfiguration that proves as powerful as the final fatal rush of hemorrhaging blood. Just before "a blind black fog swam up and closed above his head," just before "his brain faded into night," his own father appears to him in a blazing vision of immortality, bracing him with a surge of confidence at the very moment of death.

There is no scanting the gruesome physical details: the blood, the death rattle, the mass of greenish matter foaming through his lips. But the soaring beyond these to a releasing metamorphosis lends Wolfe's death scene a redemptive character as special of its kind as Tolstoy's version is of death conceived as a dreadful extinction. Wolfe's conviction of the power of life even in death accompanies Gant into his coffin. There his hands are dominant, the outsized hands of a stonecutter, looking as shapely and alive as ever. Wolfe devotes three pages of lyrical prose to describing and rhapsodizing about them.

With the departure of Gant, the book lapses back for a time into Eugene's private life. He finishes at Harvard, hoping to be a playwright and sending off the best of the plays he had written for Professor Hatcher to a producer in New York. He applies for teaching jobs at various colleges, and while waiting for the replies to all these, returns home for a long visit.

A stretch of 150 pages ensues, until the end of Book III, in which our hero assaults, with varying degrees of effectiveness, a series of favorite targets: Francis Starwick, his aesthetic Harvard friend, with his elegant affectations and carefully concealed sterility; the other students in Professor Hatcher's playwrighting class; aesthetes, art patrons, literary dabblers; poor whites, Negroes, Southern cops.

Eugene goes on a drunken spree in South Carolina and winds up in jail, cursing his captors, swearing in all directions that he will be avenged. He receives word at last that his play has been turned down, hurling him into still another fit of deep gloom. From this he is roused by news of a college teaching appointment. He bids his grieving mother farewell, leaves the South once more, and with his three years in Boston behind him, heads for New York, the "enchanted city" that has been the lodestar of all his dreams.

The trouble with these episodes—they can scarcely be called events—is that they have no perceptible effect on Eugene, the person experiencing them. He is now twenty-three, but is still exactly as he was at twenty when the novel began. Life arouses in him a tremendous emotional response, but it has become a fixed emotional response. The world around him is in perpetual motion, yet he remains absolutely still. It is not just that he does not change; he seems incapable of psychological movement of any kind. The progression evident in *Look Homeward, Angel,* loose and erratic though it was, has disappeared. This is a fact of the greatest significance. Wolfe immobilizes the internal life of his hero because that internal life is no longer his main concern.

His interest has shifted from character to scene, from psychology to panorama, from the exploration of human nature to an exploration of ecology, both physical and social. In this change of focus, Eugene undergoes radical surgery. The Eugene of *Look Homeward, Angel* not only grew up but grew. The new one has been transformed into a fixed instrument, an acetylene torch that blows red-hot but whose function is to shape something other than itself. Even in the "personal" sequences of *Of Time and the River*, our attention is drawn more readily to the brilliantly rendered passages on subjects having relatively little to do with Eugene—the slack, heavy, dangerous policemen in the small Southern towns, the hills of North Carolina in October invoked with a sonorous lyrical eloquence—than to the sporadic invective and emotion flowing out of Eugene's superheated self.

New York at last floats into view and provides Wolfe, now in full cry in his impassioned pursuit of essences, with a plummy target. Eugene reaches the great city to take up a career as teacher at the university. But not all at once, and not without a second train journey. This one does not take in the whole scene mile by mile all the way from the Smokies, but concentrates deliberately on the approaches to the supreme metropolis.

There the trains thicken in number and speed. The sense of vast clusters of people moving at great velocity toward all ends of the compass grows overwhelming. Long strings of loaded box-cars steam along at fifty miles an hour, crossing cindery roadbeds, disappearing into "the new and barren spaces of the land that ended nowhere." And at regular intervals, the reader is alerted to "the small hard light of semaphores—green, red, and yellow—as in the heart of the enormous dark they shone, for great trains smashing at the rails, their small and passionate assurances."

Entering the city itself, Eugene is struck at once by the conviction that the swarms of faces, the "blaze and sweep of the great buildings," the million-footed movement are all part of some earlier experience going back to the remote reaches of human history. Even the smaller details of the immense mosaic of New York seem like echoes and incarnations of something that has already been registered in the observer's consciousness: the thin febrile figures of the taxi drivers, the arrogant, knowing, beak-nosed Jews, the heavy-figured Irish cops with their red beefy faces, the whole mongrel compost of city life—as Wolfe's yeasty verbiage would have it— appear "to be fixed in something classic, and eternal, in the everlasting variousness and fixity of time."

The persuasive combination of these opposite elements— the legendary and the familiar, the changing and the immemorial, what is happening now with its overpowering novelty sheathing the fact of its perpetual recurrence— supplies New York as it bursts into life in these pages with its peculiar potency and splendor. Having blocked out the forms of the city, Eugene proceeds to ingest them. Once he gets the city into his insides, it will never be able to escape him:

> He saw the city with the great giant webbing of its thousand streets . . . six million sleepers celled in sleep and walled in night, and girdled by the bracelet of two flashing seaborne tides that isled them round: he held them legible as minted gold within his hand, he saw them plain as apples in the adyts of his brain . . . his hunger could eat the earth, his eye and brain gulp down the vision of ten thousand streets, ten million faces, he knew he should . . . eat them all one day.

The movement from the individual to the general proceeds with erratic persistency. Eugene begins teaching and is conscious at once of how Jewish his students are. Their physical presence oppresses him. He cannot stand their swarthiness, their noisy and aggressive intelligence, even the unpleasant way they sweat. One of them, Abraham Jones, breaks through the emotional barrier and establishes a kind of friendship and intimacy with Eugene. But the Jewish foreignness and darkness, their city hardness, are qualities Eugene cannot assimilate. He can manage them in his imagination, however, if not in their immediate classroom presence, by defining them as a force in history, patient, suffering, long-enduring, tempered by endless crises. Abraham Jones's aging mother is transformed from a toothless old woman into a female, "timeless, ageless, fixed in sorrow and fertility . . . as enduring and fecund as the earth." Her face "was unmistakably the face of an old Jewess and yet the powerful and craggy features bore an astonishing resemblance to the face of a pioneer woman or of an old Indian chief."

As he shifts the Jews from the immediate moment to the longer context of history by changing them from a throng of visible persons pressing upon him to the abstraction of a folk, it is possible for him to keep his disturbed feelings under some sort of control. The whole new surge of Wolfe's art from the particular to the representational keeps him from drowning in a self-generating flood of virulent anti-Semitism. The aesthetic mechanism that enables Wolfe to admire and even love the Jews while continuing to hate and fear them reveals itself not simply as a literary process but as an act of necessary therapy.

In describing New York, Wolfe is much more at home as a writer with those whom Eugene meets collectively than with those whom he knows as individuals. The city crowds, the faces and scenes caught through train windows, the urban Jews seen up close and then distanced through the eye of history, are effective, at times triumphant sequences. But when Eugene's college friends appear, drifting back into his life at carefully spaced intervals, the results are depressing, even disastrous. One such friend, Robert Weaver, spends chapters 50 and 54 in Eugene's New York hotel, thrashing about with his mistress and her enraged tubercular husband. The effect is pure tabloid; Wolfe's purpose in pouring so much energy into this squalid incident remains baffling.

Another friend, Joel Pierce, appears; he leads Wolfe into a blind alley that lasts for a hundred tiresome pages. His family occupies a luxurious estate on the Hudson River to which he brings Eugene as a house guest. This is Eugene's—and Wolfe's—first exposure to the rich, and he does not quite know how to behave, what attitude to assume toward them, or what tone to adopt. Later on, in *You Can't Go Home Again*, Wolfe will profit from this experience when he depicts the Jacks in their wealthy Fifth Avenue milieu. Here, among the Pierces, he betrays his nervousness and uncertainty by jumping back and forth between glamorous idealization and heavy satire. Neither is effective. When Eugene listens to his friend's beautiful young sister talk about her desire to have a great life, he is thrilled beyond measure, though vaguely irked because she is engaged to be married. Yet his romantic emotion is lopsided; it rests entirely within himself; the girl is too shadowy and unsubstantial a figure to generate anything in her own right.

By contrast, the mother, Mrs. Pierce, is treated very harshly and satirically; her haughtiness, snobbery, social self-assurance, and condescension are recorded by a young man who suffers from them. We are made to feel that she is not being observed disinterestedly, but that Eugene, angered and embarrassed by the small humiliations she inflicts upon him, forces her into tedious caricature to relieve his own injured feelings. Poised neatly, perhaps too neatly, between mother and daughter, is the grandfather, a stiff-backed archetype of the gentleman aristocrat who incarnates the spirit of the region he inhabits.

Yet what a region it is, and what justice Wolfe does to it. The Hudson River valley, particularly by moonlight, extracts from him some of his most eloquent and persuasive prose. Here his as yet halting and deficient sense of social observation is not required to operate. The evocation of landscape, as Eugene strolls about the lawns and hillsides with the younger Pierces, is one of those "natural" acts that Wolfe performs with effortless skill. It does not matter whether the landscape is empty of people as in the Hudson River tableaux or crowded with them as in New York City, whether he is observing it from a motionless position or from a speeding train. The results are invariably splendid. It is a pity that Wolfe died before the moon landings. His descriptive powers had an extraterrestrial quality superbly suited to grappling with the awesome landscape of outer space. And his hunger to encompass everything—on earth and beyond—might at last have found its ultimate object.

A vast block of three hundred pages still remains in this longest of Wolfe's novels. He uses all of them for a running account of Eugene's first journey to Europe. Our hero gets no deeper into the Old World than England and France. Germany, the absolute country of Wolfe's soul, still lies ahead and will not be reached until the later books and in the person of a later hero. But France and England supply Eugene with enough material to feed upon, indeed to gorge himself on. Once again the split in the book is manifest: between Eugene as Wolfe's instrument of observation and Eugene living his own private life, between the voyage as an exploration of the world and the voyage as a mechanism to evolve the drama of self, between Europe as canvas to be painted and Europe as a picturesque backdrop to the emotions of the traveler.

Once again it is what Eugene sees and chronicles with the observer's eye that is effective and enduring, and what he experiences on the personal side that is tedious and hollow. *Of Time and the River*, to its very end and with accelerating speed and visibility, lapses in that part of itself which is a novel and achieves a kind of triumph in that part which goes outside the bounds of traditional fiction and takes hold of life in those aspects beyond the immediate narrative moment.

First, there is England: "Smoke-gold by day, the numb exultant secrecies of fog . . . an ancient yellow light, the old smoke-ochre of the morning, never coming to an open brightness." This swift articulation of light and weather is followed by a rapid and generally illuminating commentary on English manners, physique, pronunciation, food, family life, the appearance of college towns, the "huge smoky web" of London, the feel and grain of the country. All of it rendered in a kaleidoscope of quick impressions unreeling before us with an impressive fluency. It is not easy to write a good travelogue. One requires a highly developed visual sense and a strong feeling for composition. Wolfe is clearly endowed with both, making him an excellent person to have along on any sort of journey. Accenting and solidifying his art are all those brilliantly defined voyages by train, boat, car, and, in the great cities, on foot in which his unique powers as an energized painter of scene are given free play.

In France the results are equally telling. There are two ways of responding to that difficult country: with slavish adulation of the French or by poking fun at their overdeveloped qualities. Wolfe chooses the second. Eugene is soon to meet Francis Starwick again, full of half-Frenchified manners and affectations—a painful example of how destructive adulation, when inadequately grounded, can be. So he proceeds to tease the French, and on their own terms, without making a cosmic occasion of it. Within this modest framework, traveling light as it were, he gets off his good-natured raillery very well and so eases his way into a new country.

He begins by running through the names of French writers, not the well-known ones like Stendhal, Balzac, and Flaubert, but obscure second- and third-raters of whom no American would ordinarily have heard. They ripple off the tongue like cream, the very smooth Frenchiness of their names establishing the satirical point: everybody in French literature seems to write well, down to the most minor, most obscure provincial essayist. How do they do it? muses our American visitor. He then launches into a charming—and funny—little fantasy about how they all sit around cafés and, amid the din of traffic, write their beautiful creamy little sentences, carrying on neat, effortless conversations with one another in perfect harmony, writing their unread little masterpieces untroubled by conditions and distractions that would disintegrate the efforts of writers living in the great outside world that is not France.

From time to time Wolfe zeroes in on French faces, Parisian women with their "hard avaricious noses" and "enamelled tinted skin." He spins around Paris with the same ferocious velocity with which he rammed his way at Harvard through the Widener Library, and winds up paying tribute to the city in language equal in eloquence to Henry James's celebrated outbursts on the same subject: "Great circle, unending universe of life, huge legend of dark time!"

Up to this point, almost seven hundred pages deep into the book, *Of Time and the River* has been a work of startling interest and originality, profoundly different in its internal movements and directions from *Look Homeward, Angel*. Now Eugene, as hero of the novel, elbows the other Eugene, Eugene the impassioned observer, offstage, and for the greater part of the next two hundred pages afflicts us again with the tedious drama of his personal life. The details need not detain us long, though they are skeined out at elaborate length. Eugene resumes his relationship with Starwick and becomes involved with two young women from Boston who have attached themselves to Starwick: Eugene falls in love with the younger.

The four knock about Paris night and day. They are happy; they quarrel; tensions arise among them in hard little nodules of frustrated energy. After "doing" Paris, they pile into a car and roam around the French countryside. There are good moments, but the emotions worsen steadily; misunderstandings mount; rage increases; and at last everything blows sky-high in the ultimate revelation that Starwick is homosexual. None of this is very interesting in itself: the narrative is animated enough, but it moves in steadily narrower rather than wider circles and soon begins to feed upon itself, a cannibalizing process that Wolfe is unable to control.

For all the heavily charged emotional content of the whole protracted sequence, there are virtually no psychological perceptions, no insights into character, none of those little nuggets of wisdom that unexpectedly appear in the texts of fine novelists. And at the end Eugene is exactly where he was at the beginning, not only unchanged but not even very much the worse for wear. The reader in fact has undergone a

severer trial than he, and has suffered considerably more than
the hero for all his "suffering."

Swampy though much of this is, groaning with heavy-fisted
love scenes in which the characters declaim to one another in
the rigid stances of nineteenth-century melodrama, there are
touches and moments of the other Wolfe that flash across the
gray, gluey scene. On a train to Paris he once again, through
Eugene's eyes, resumes his effective role as Peeping Tom. He
looks in on the houses along the track, sees a boy leaning on a
table reading a book, a woman unhooking a canary birdcage
hanging in the window.

Still on the train, he projects in his imagination a series of
visions in an expanding cornucopia: individuals merge into
trains steaming past; the trains converge upon a boat train,
groomed and opulent, heading for the Channel ports; the
boat train changes into a "huge, white-breasted" ocean liner
whose "terrific stacks" are soon to drive it across the Atlantic
in a dreamlike world of wealth and pleasure. The ship leaves;
the coast of France, "braceleted" with "hard, spare lights,"
recedes in the distance; and far ahead America looms up,
America in the shape of Manhattan: "The spires and
ramparts of the enfabled isle, the legendary and aerial smoke,
the stone and steel, of the terrific city." In stretches of this
kind, Wolfe barges ahead toward his ultimate destination as a
writer, seizing the movements of earth and man.

The coda of this immense second book opens with one of
Wolfe's famous passages, a short swing through history and
time in a mixture of high seriousness and low parody touched
off by the words, "Play us a tune on an unbroken spinet."
This leads into the theme of home, the wanderer in Europe

returning home. The ache of home launches Wolfe into another animated ramble through the landscape of American names: rivers, Indian tribes, states, railroad lines, battles, mountains, winding up with a social register of the great American tramps from Oklahoma Red and Fargo Pete to Dixie Joe and the Jersey Dutchman.

He asks the question, "For what are we, my brother?" and delivers his cosmic answer, "We are a phantom flare of grieved desire, the ghostling and phosphoric flicker of immortal time, a brevity of days haunted by the eternity of the earth." Scarcely an original answer, but expressed with an energy so breathtaking and in language so hauntingly beautiful as to turn it into a soaring and irresistible truth.

Eugene is at last ready to return home. Sitting in a Dijon square, watching the French shuffling home from work, all he can think of are late afternoons in Altamont twenty years before when, as a small boy standing in front of his father's shop in the town square, he watched the men shuffling home from work. He remembers the screen doors that slammed behind them and the "sudden silence"—in that earlier America of quiet streets and leafy fragrance before it sank beneath the overwhelming blast of the new industrial age. If in Europe all he can think of is America, it is plainly time for him to leave.

He makes his way to Cherbourg, boards the boat that will take him back to his own country, and there meets a rich American woman much older than himself with whom he falls instantly in love. Together they set sail for New York, "the fabulous rock of life, the proud, masted city of the soaring towers, which was flung with a lion's port into the maw of ocean." She is Jewish, like the Aline Bernstein of real life, and as the ocean liner gets under way, this leads to the last blazing sentence of the book: "Proud, potent faces of rich Jews, alive with wealth and luxury, glow in rich, lighted cabins; the doors are closed, and the ship is given to the darkness and the sea."

At long last, having lunged forward to page 912 before finally coming to a halt, one of the more exultant literary adventures of our times has come to an end.

The profound effect *Of Time and the River* had upon Wolfe himself is indicated by the striking fact that he was moved to write a book on how he wrote it. Of his four novels, this was the only one to rate that much separate attention from him. He called the memoir *The Story of a Novel.* In this revealing little gloss, Wolfe sums up the theme of his huge second work: "I wrote about night and darkness in America, and the faces of the sleepers in ten thousand little towns; and of the tides of sleep and how the rivers flowed forever in the darkness. . . . I wrote about death and sleep, and of that enfabled rock of life we call the city. I wrote about October, of great trains that thundered through the night, of ships and stations in the morning; of men in harbors and the traffic of the ships."

Significantly, there is nothing here about Eugene Gant or the familiar materials and forms of fiction. After it was finished, *Of Time and the River* began to appear in the author's mind, perhaps for the first time, as a watershed in his creative life. Seen thus, it was an error to regard it as an erratic, incoherent, disorganized, chaotic novel that did not know where it was going. Instead it demands to be regarded as a radical, if as yet incomplete, point of departure toward a form of art seeking to express not individual characters and particularized social situations but the altogether different categories represented by such terms as night, rivers, death, sleep, cities, ships, and October.

Wolfe goes on in *The Story of a Novel* to describe himself in the grip of three kinds of time—present, past, and immutable: "Time immutable, the time of rivers, mountains, oceans, and the earth; a kind of eternal and unchanging universe of time against which would be projected the transience of man's life, the bitter briefness of his day." *Of Time and the River* is a sustained attempt to turn the temporal into the eternal, to find some way of funneling the first two time categories into the massive permanence of the third.

This aim is signaled formally by the mythological tags, both ancient and modern, given to the eight parts of the novel: these include the names of men like Orestes, Jason, and Faust and of gods like Proteus and Antaeus; they go back to the remote beginning of time with Kronos and Rhea, the parents of Zeus himself. This is a deliberate effort to plug Eugene and the passing flux of past and present time into an immortal and unchanging circuit, and Wolfe is willing to risk being thought pretentious in order to announce and anchor his larger intention in the very table of contents of his work.

If read as a standard novel, *Of Time and the River* is a busted-up, every-which-way sort of book, quite awful. But it is quite wonderful if taken as a pursuit of the far perspective of time, as a thrilling first stage in which Wolfe is shucking off his original trappings and, snakelike, struggling to create a new skin. That it was only a first stage is suggested by Perkins's radical intervention in calling an abrupt halt to *Of Time and the River* while Wolfe was rushing on to ever-widening piles of material. While still in the midst of the book, his projection of what lay ahead had already assumed

the following monumental terms: "It was not until . . . I
realized finally that what I had to deal with was material
which covered almost 150 years in history, demanded the
action of more than 2000 characters, and would in its final
design include almost every racial type and social class of
American life, that I realized that even the pages of a book of
200,000 words were wholly inadequate for the purpose."

In the grandiosity and bulk of this swelling ambition,
Wolfe recalled the universe-swallowing Whitman, Eugene
O'Neill with his unfinished eleven-play cycle going back to
the American beginnings, and naturalists like Theodore
Dreiser with their compulsively documentary recording of
every last detail. Yet quantity as such was not what Wolfe
was after: "I really believe that so far as the artist is
concerned, the unlimited extent of human experience is not
so important for him as the depth and intensity with which
he experiences things." Just as he seeks to hook transient time
into immutable time, so he seeks to harness bulk with depth.
He draws energy from the world, but in the end merges it
with his own energy in a titanic fusion appropriate to the
range and size of his subjects.

Of Time and the River is not a finished piece of work. Its
genius lies precisely in the fact that it is not finished, that in
its deep internal division between the old form of narrative
and the new it emerges as a book of strikingly separable
sections, of gigantic fragments. Its interest is thus intensely
dramatic. It is the salient crossroads, the great battleground
of Wolfe's emerging art.

4

The Web and the Rock

꧁꧂ At first glance, this third book seems to be *Look Homeward, Angel* all over again. Like Oliver Gant, the father—John Webber—comes down from the North to the South, marries a local girl with crowds of relatives, and the marriage doesn't work. Webber is a brickmaker, not so very different from Gant the stonecutter, and the town of Libya Hill looks like a duplicate of Altamont. But the resemblance is illusory. Wolfe goes all the way back to the beginning, to be sure, but only to run a different kind of race.

Where *Look Homeward, Angel* centers around the family, in *The Web and the Rock* George Webber is deliberately stripped of the usual family ties. His father goes off to live with another woman when he is still a small boy, and his mother dies soon after. An only child, he is brought up by an elderly aunt, and is in fact alone in the world, removed from father and mother, and devoid of siblings. The day-by-day, blow-by-blow growth of Eugene within the frame of a highly dramatic, intensely complicated, and incredibly noisy family situation is utterly absent here. George seems to grow up in a vacuum. Indeed he does not appear in the story at first hand until he is twelve years old.

The characteristic quality of Eugene's boyhood is din; of George's, silence. This is reflected in the prose. The first novel opens in ecstasy, with grandiloquent time sweeps and much palpitating rhetoric. The third begins soberly, with a quiet, restrained, almost documentary tone, as though a journalist rather than a novelist were at work. Factual sentences like these, all but invisible in *Look Homeward, Angel,* bestrew the opening paragraphs: "In the main, those facts are correct." "Aside from that, it is worth noting that Mr. Webber had his friends." "The railroad was then being built and would soon be finished." "The bare anatomy of the story runs as follows."

Hitherto, the bare anatomy of anything was foreign to Wolfe. His energies ran to fleshing everything to the point of opulence. Now he strives for detachment, thinks of his present writing as "a genuine spiritual and artistic change," and even writes an Author's Note to tell us that this is so. In any event, the whole first chapter is as lean and terse as anything he ever wrote, almost as though he had gone through the regimen prescribed for him by Hemingway in *Green Hills of Africa*: "I wonder if it would make a writer of him, give him the necessary shock to cut the over-flow of words and give him a sense of proportion, if they sent Tom Wolfe to Siberia or to the Dry Tortugas."

It takes Eugene a couple of hundred pages to reach the age of twelve, by which time his growth and character have been minutely detailed. George gets there by page 13, at which point we know something about his family connections but about him hardly anything at all. In Chapter 2, "Three O'Clock," we find George sprawled on the grass in front of his aunt's house at three in the afternoon, sunk in an extended daydream.

None of it has very much to do with himself. The chapter is a potpourri of thoughts and comments on a large number of subjects of great interest to Wolfe and only vaguely related to George: North Carolina as a better place than South Carolina; the odiousness of poor whites; the web as a metaphor for his mother's family, the rock for his father's; three o'clock on a golden afternoon, a peak of human existence from which one ought not to be roused by calls to trivial duty; the difference—among his boyhood companions—between adolescent clots like Ira, Dock, and Reese and the admirable and heroic Nebraska Crane.

George is primarily a device to get all these sketched in. As an observer he refracts very few of them on his own. Wolfe is proceeding inexorably on the path of using his fiction to paint states of mind, social landscapes, and ecological sprawls. George Webber, even more than the later Eugene, is the chief instrument to this end in the third and fourth novels, a much more adequate instrument because little energy is diverted to setting him up as an individual personality with complex requirements of his own and his own special ways of looking at things.

He is given a genealogy, a life history, an occupation as a writer when he grows up, a distinctive physical appearance—long-armed, simian, causing him to be nicknamed "Monk," Wolfe going to elaborate pains to make him look as different from Eugene as possible—and an ego of sorts that is later to erupt in quite inexplicable fits of fury. But aside from one extended love affair, he is given no private self, none of that stitchwork of individual traits that lead to the remembered character, very little even of the quirkiness and eccentricity that so often passes for characterization. George Webber is to become Wolfe's highly advanced tool, not for the writing of novels but for the recording of his feelings, images, and visions of life.

In *The Web and the Rock* such visions lean to the grotesque. George feels within himself a blood madness, which he attributes to a hereditary taint in his mother's family. These mountain people, the Joyners, isolated and inbred, hopelessly webbed in an unfathomable, slow-smoldering past, are sunk in a huge abyss of "drowning time," in "a sea of blind, dateless Joyner time," and have left him with an infection of the soul.

What all this means exactly is not wholly clear. What Wolfe is creating is less a rational structure than a state of mind, an intensely impressionistic sense of psychic sludge, suppuration, murkiness, out of which will rise, like a Grendel from the dark sea, outbursts of rage and violence. Much of this is beyond the range of coherent expression; once again Wolfe is pressing and forcing language to seize what is almost outside its power to do. Yet it is in this zone where the clear becomes translucent, and the translucent slopes off into the opaque, that Wolfe is most at home and achieves one of his resourceful triumphs as a writer.

The dark genealogical strain in George is matched, perhaps even signaled, by a series of grotesque episodes that begin on a small scale, then reach a plateau of pure horror. He is given to amusingly queer little superstitions, like doing everything in patterns and groupings of four or picking a different human organ to stare at on each day of the week—other people's noses one day, ears the second, mouths the third, and so on. This odd behavior soon leads into far more serious events, though they have nothing to do with George directly except that he witnesses them.

There is the incident of the two boys run over by an automobile, with brains and entrails scattered over the pavement and Wolfe pouncing, with sudden savagery, on the gruesome details. Nobody is actually killed in the next scene, which presents the butcher and his family, but its four members, the mastodonic, mind-crushing mother especially, are pathological monsters straight out of the naturalist bin of Zola and Maupassant. This whole sequence of exercises in the grotesque is climaxed by the stunningly executed chapter, "The Child by Tiger," in which Dick Prosser, a Negro ex-soldier, runs amok, and after killing a number of his pursuers with splendid military precision, is himself killed, badly mutilated, and finally immortalized in a thrilling requiem: "He came out of the heart of darkness, from the dark heart of the secret and undiscovered South. . . . He was night's child and partner . . . a symbol of man's evil innocence . . . a friend, a brother, and a mortal enemy."

If, as Thomas Mann asserted, the grotesque is the characteristic mode of twentieth-century art, then Wolfe is very much a writer of his time. To him the grotesque, however, is not something that lies on the visible surface of things, like graffiti covering the sides of trains on the New York subway. It is instead a force in nature, a current of energy hidden from view, erupting at irregular intervals and usually when least expected.

One goes along with the ordinary, the familiar, the normal, lulled into the conviction that this is the animating principle of the universe, when an explosion from within blows everything apart. The normal becomes abnormal; the ordinary, extraordinary; the rules of the commonplace and the routine suffer a severe internal convulsion and break into fragments. The grotesque is the disintegrative element hidden in the normal, the Mr. Hyde lurking within Dr. Jekyll's civilized appearance, as indigenous to the order of nature as the process of integration and wholeness in which, in fact, it is absurdly embedded as a prankish and malevolent twin.

So that as George is walking along the all too familiar main street of Libya Hill, there comes the rocketing smash of the two boys. As he enters the commonplace butcher shop on a routine errand, he hears the subhuman voice of the butcher's wife relating her frightful beating of her six-foot daughter to punish the girl for "sinning," followed without pause by the butcher's voice threatening to murder his embezzling and absconding son should he ever return.

And the bloody saga of Dick Prosser is prefaced by his normal conduct before he goes berserk: courteous, attentive, deeply religious, beautifully instructing the young white boys in making a fire, boxing, marksmanship, football, and all the manly arts. So that when, for obscure reasons, he goes mad, the terrible destruction that follows is all the more terrible because it flows organically out of its opposite principle. Wolfe manages and executes this theory and genre of the grotesque with great dexterity. This represents for him a reigning aspect of the world as constituted. To the very end, *The Web and the Rock* is the work in which it most forcefully operates, which supplies its most luminous illustrations.

George Webber's formative years pass very quickly, with himself not much in evidence. His uncle takes him on long walks in the mountains and douses him with lengthy folktales about the Joyners. Presently he is sixteen and in college, the same college Eugene and Wolfe began attending at the same age. The four college years are telescoped into a handful of special moments: a football hero whom the school worships; George's discovery of Dostoevsky; a lone professor who makes an impression on him; some casual satire on flaccid academic bromides about service to humanity while hardship and poverty on a mass scale go on undisturbed; enthusiasm for the First World War, and how all the young men longed to fight in it and hated to see it end. Again the focus is on the general rather than the particular, on commonly shared attitudes toward commonly shared experiences: war, sports, literature, suffering mankind, and the academic life. Any young man of reasonably open mind could have exchanged places with George in these pages, and the result would have been largely the same.

Eugene and George are the same personality types, young writers of explosive genius who are very full of themselves, but where Eugene is encouraged to express himself on his own terms, and in *Look Homeward, Angel* without restraints of any kind, George is kept in check, and through the first half of *The Web and the Rock* severely so. Wolfe is quite right in claiming in his Author's Note: "This novel marks not only a turning away from the books I have written in the past, but a genuine spiritual and artistic change. It is the most objective novel that I have written." The artistic change began taking place, as we have seen, in *Of Time and the River*, and is now in full operation. And what Wolfe means by "objective" is not quite what the reader senses. He is referring to created figures in the novel who are drawn directly from his own life. The reader sees Wolfe's "objectivity" less here than in his representation of the characteristically general rather than the uniquely particular.

With what for him is remarkable speed, Wolfe gets George through college in North Carolina and up to Manhattan, where he is finally launched as a writer. We learn even less of George in the act of writing than we did of Eugene. He seems always to be either about to write or to have just written.

While he is trying to get on as a writer, he earns his living as a teacher—as did Eugene. We at least witnessed Eugene in the act of teaching. He *was* in the classroom, with students before him of whose presence and race he was all too conscious. George is never seen teaching. His classes are off somewhere in the middle distance; they never appear onstage. About all that we get are some sneers at New York University. George dubs it the School for Utility Cultures, an educational factory manned by grubby, mean-spirited, sterile faculty members whose only aim is to get promoted, whose principal emotion is envy, and whose favorite weapon is backbiting. Thus his teaching, even more than his writing, turns out to be a cover for other matters, a formality to give George something to do while Wolfe grapples with subjects more vital to him.

One of these is New York or, as the sociological cant phrase puts it, the urban experience. If anything can be said to anchor Wolfe's imaginative energies, it is the great city. It is never far from his thoughts, fantasies, and longings, and keeps surfacing even when his mind is occupied with other business. New York is the enfabled rock, the only arena that can realize his dream of greatness, the shining tower of the North luring him from his remote birthplace in the South, the supreme climax of the country, pivotal to "the plantations of the earth." Upon it he lavishes some of his most voluptuous prose, not always in love and admiration, often in anger and disdain, but unfailingly with a compelled fascination that never slackens. *The Web and the Rock*, and after it *You Can't Go Home Again*, are primarily soul outbursts about the glittering American megalopolis.

As George approaches the city for the first time, Wolfe's epithets become as gracefully expressive as the Manhattan skyline itself. "That ship of life, that swarming, million-footed, tower-masted, and sky-soaring citadel . . . . the gigantic tenement of Here Comes Everybody." The city is real, yet unreal. It holds forth the promise of fame, yet supplies a cloak of instant anonymity. "It offers all, and yet it offers nothing. It gives to every man a home, and it is the great No Home of the earth."

Wolfe is eloquent about the different seasons in New York, responds to the "green sorcery" of April, and rises to particular splendor with winter: "On one of those nights of frozen silence when the cold is so intense that it numbs one's flesh, and the sky above the city flashes with one deep jewelry of cold stars, the whole city, no matter how ugly its parts may be . . . seems to soar up with an aspirant, vertical, glittering magnificence to meet the stars. One hears the hoarse notes of the great ships in the river, and one remembers suddenly the princely girdle of proud, potent tides that bind the city, and suddenly New York blazes like a magnificent jewel in its fit setting of sea, and earth, and stars." It even has its own special odors: "The odor of a dynamo . . . of electricity, . . . the odor of the cellar, of an old brick house or of a city building, closed, a little stale and dank, touched with a subtle, fresh, half-rotten smell of harbor."

Wolfe's special vantage point is that he is an outsider to the city, an entranced outsider to be sure, but an outsider to the last. He is never fully at home in it, never quite at ease. It is always a foreign country to be conquered. Among those novelists who grow up in the cities they write about, the city is always there, an intimate, familiar, and assumed presence. Dickens is frequently conscious of London but seldom self-conscious about it. Joyce does not have to rhapsodize about Dublin; it is too instinctive a part of him. There is no space between Dostoevsky and the St. Petersburg where young Raskolnikov commits his crimes and undergoes his fevered resurrection. Studs Lonigan and Chicago are one. The characters in Edward Lewis Wallant, perhaps the ultimate urban novelist in our literature, embody the New York slums and near slums which they inhabit; when they leave them for whatever reason, they seem like displaced persons.

By contrast, Wolfe is the eternal visitor, the perpetual, super-alert tourist. He is forever grabbing Manhattan and Brooklyn (and to a lesser degree London, Paris, Berlin, and Munich) by the scruff of the neck and exclaiming to us, How marvelous! or, How awful! He is always *discovering* the city, colliding with it in quick ecstatic encounters, observing it as an exotic phenomenon. Wolfe has a great advantage in this over the native writer in terms of sheer level of awareness. He never takes the city for granted, never loses his sense of wonder, is always on the *qui vive*, his antennae bristlingly alive.

> The hoof and the wheel went by upon the street, as they had done forever, the manswarm milled and threaded in the stupefaction of the streets, and the high, immortal sound of time, murmurous and everlasting,

brooded forever in the upper air above the fabulous walls and towers of the city.

Wolfe forces us, particularly those who have grown up in the city, to see it through eyes that are perpetually fresh because they are always foreign. When we return from travel abroad, our hometown seems shockingly new; for an interval, the familiar has become radically unfamiliar before it gradually lapses back into its original shape. What Wolfe does is to memorialize that interval, and compel us to see our habitat as though we were seeing it for the first time. One can extrapolate his outbursts about New York and present them as a sequence of highly intensified bas-reliefs, almost as an art form in themselves distinct from other elements in his books. In this instance, as in so many others, he fulfills the ancient role of the artist; he reveals the world in a transcendent light.

But Wolfe tackles the city not only in terms of epic impressionism. He also sees it as the source, the breeder, the nurturing ground of certain social types who by their very nature can flourish nowhere else. One of these is the Jews, seen here not from below as in *Of Time and the River* where Eugene was confronted in the classroom by the sons and daughters of struggling East Side immigrants. They are observed from above, the wealthy Jews who have made it to Park Avenue and arouse in George an admiration for their energy, their opulence, their love of good food, and their refusal to put up with the second rate. The fear of being dominated by them both spiritually and sexually is still present in him but only as a quietly though persistently throbbing undertone.

Another of Wolfe's urban categories is the rich. For them he reserves some of his more ferocious condemnations. They throw their money around like ostentatious grandees while the masses of people groan in squalor. They "take up" and patronize artists and art, not out of any genuine feeling for culture or the creative process but as ego gratification, as fads or toys to feed their vanity and sense of power.

Yet he shares Fitzgerald's conviction that the rich are different from other people: "Just as their garments are of the finest and richest textures, so the texture of their flesh . . . and all their combining sinews, tissues, and ligaments are fairer and finer than those of poorer people." Still, it is better to know rich people than to be rich oneself, and "it is not wealth but the thought of wealth that is wonderful." Some cautionary instinct kept Wolfe from sliding into the abyss of money hunger in which the Fitzgeralds at last drowned.

Yet another figure whose lot is tied to the city is the artist. The urban sprawl generates all those complex forms of human experience which nourish his imagination. Within it there cluster the publishers, galleries, orchestras, museums that discover, display, and market his wares. It supplies the patrons who sponsor his work, the flocks of aesthetes who feed off it, the critics who from Wolfe's point of view exist only to attack and destroy it like ticks bloating themselves on the blood of other organisms.

George Webber, in his role as aspiring writer, is always throwing himself at the city in an effort to swallow it and its secrets whole. At the same time, almost in the same breath, he is defending himself against the hordes of natural enemies whom he regards as conspiring to bring him down: insensitive publishers (like the house of Rawng and Wright—one of Wolfe's clumsier satirical contraptions), egotistical art patrons, celebrity-hunting women, carnivorous book reviewers, self-important schools of critics, aesthetic dilettantes formulating fashionable attitudes, and all the fakers, poseurs, and would-be artists cluttering up the urban landscape. "He saw them all—the enervate rhapsodists of jazz, the Wastelanders, Humanists, Expressionists, Surrealists, Neo-primitives, and Literary Communists."

In such persistently dramatic terms, Wolfe conceives the struggle within the city for the soul of man and the integrity of the artist. As the source of experience and perhaps even ultimate wisdom, the city is the great rock. As the breeder of viruses dangerous to body and mind, it is the great web. Thus the metaphor embedded in the title of the book provides it with the positive and negative poles between which everything oscillates.

As another example of this polarized movement, and of Wolfe's fascinating if eccentric sociology, is his flat division of human beings into two spiritual groups: those who have richness and joy in them and those who have not. Among the first are prize fighters, policemen, racing drivers, locomotive engineers, steel workers, all the physical and active people. Among the second are those who rustle papers or tap keys, clerks, college instructors, people who eat lunch in drugstores, who live meagerly and in pale safety. After this, it would take a very bold reader indeed ever to allow himself to be caught eating lunch in a drugstore even if in his heart he believes that Wolfe's social categories are nonsensical.

Nonsensical or not, they are an attempt to cast light on the quality of life, on essential movements of the human spirit which in Wolfe's view are felt more forcefully in the city than elsewhere. In the end, his very images of good and evil are twined at the core of megalopolis. In language suggestive of Conrad describing the Congo winding its way to the heart of Africa or the telegraph wires in *Nostromo* coiling like tentacles through Costaguana, Wolfe describes the shocking impact of evil upon his hero.

He has come upon it abruptly in the midtown streets after the Dempsey-Firpo fight where milling thousands of vicious men, "the criminal visages of the night," snarled and screamed their raging disappointment. "Suddenly it seemed to Monk that a great snake lay coiled at the very heart and center of the city's life, that a malevolent and destructive energy was terribly alive and working there, and that he and the others who had come here from the little towns and from the country places, with such high passion and with so much hope, were confronted now with something evil and unknown at the heart of life, which they had not expected, and for which all of them were unprepared."

The Web and the Rock is Wolfe's ode to the city which brought his art, as it did his life, to its climax.

Wolfe's love-hate affair with New York is carried on simultaneously in George's affair with Mrs. Jack. She, like the Aline Bernstein of real life, is seen by her young lover as the embodiment of the urban spirit, and he is indeed drawn to her as much by that as by her personal charms. He has been lured out of his Southern town by the promise of fame. He is attracted to Esther Jack because she is already established, successful, and famous. She knows the city with the intimacy of a native, an intimacy George longs to acquire. She seems to know its special secrets, how the city works, how to manipulate the machinery of success, and as a part of their lovemaking, George pumps her without letup, seeking to shake all that she knows out of her in order that he may absorb it into himself.

When things are going well between them and their love

thrives, he feels exhilarated about the city, loses his sense of impotence at being one human atom among millions, and is certain that he will triumph. At such times he regards Mrs. Jack as the incarnation of the city at its best:

> She was full of joy, tenderness, and lively humor, and she was immensely brave and gentle. He saw plainly that she was a product of the city. She had been born in the city, lived in it all her life, and she loved it; and yet she didn't have the harassed and driven look, the sallow complexion, the strident and metallic quality that many city people have. She was the natural growth of steel, stone, and masonry, yet she was as fresh, juicy, and rosy as if she had come out of the earth.

When things go badly between them, he blames not only her but the city, whose hostile and destructive side she now represents. Whatever the emotional climate, she is one in his eyes with the city from which she springs. In loving her and hating her, his real target is New York. Again it is characteristic of Wolfe's art—particularly the art of his growing maturity—that he sees the personal element in larger terms, that he transfers even the intimacy of a love affair to a frame of reference far greater than itself.

Like Virgil leading Dante into the circles of the Inferno, Mrs. Jack guides George Webber through the labyrinth of New York. As a set designer, she is privy to the secrets of the theatre. She takes him up front and backstage, while he devours hungrily all sides of this peculiarly urban phenomenon: its atmosphere, substance, tone, craft, everything that she exposes to his avid gaze. Her guided tour feeds his love for her; he is consumed with admiration for her at-homeness in all this glamour, and at the same time it feeds the black side of his nature by arousing in him clouds of jealousy over her "success" and a compulsive desire to expose the "phoniness" of these tinsel surroundings.

Wolfe is not interested in the theatre as such. Mrs. Jack is always designing sets for one play or another, but we never do get to see the plays unfolding or the actors playing or the scenes being rehearsed; for that matter, we do not even get to see the sets. Mrs. Jack is forever working over them in a little corner of George's room which she has transformed into a model of neatness and efficiency in contrast to the chaotic disarray of George's area. It is the artist *at* work rather than the artist's work which is the target. It is not the theatre but the ambience and the feeling of the theatre that are brought into focus. Again Wolfe is not after facts, he is after essences; and the facts are only the anteroom through which he must pass to get at his ultimate object.

Mrs. Jack is also a fashion designer for one of the elegant New York establishments, and when she is not working up sets for a new play, she is busy sketching the new styles. She thus has entrée to another of Manhattan's distinctive institutions, the garment industry, and along with it the great department stores and the merchandising world. George is greedy for all this special knowledge, which she willingly siphons into him in the most leisurely and abundant detail. The flow between them—her supplying and his receiving—is as much an act of love as their physical embrace, and it arouses both their natures to an absolute pitch. Her supreme pleasure is to give, just as his is to absorb, to swallow, and indeed to swallow up. So she offers up to him all her assembled experience, all her inside information, and this is the fuel that keeps their love affair rocketing along.

It is when he has emptied her of what she knows, when he has extracted from her all her secrets, pockets of intimacy, private revelations about New York, that their relationship begins to falter, stumble, and go downhill. In the end, when this essential supply of energy runs dry, he is to cast her aside like a squeezed-out lemon. Brutal certainly, with a shattering effect upon her, but logical, and on the emotional side, inevitable.

The conquest of Mrs. Jack, seen as the conquest of the great city, runs along a multitude of other lines. She and George are bound together by the very drama of the anonymous, teeming streets. They take long walks in which they swap heated impressions that literally radiate from them as they move. The massive assault upon the senses evoked by even a casual stroll through the city intoxicates them beyond measure, and they never feel closer together or love one another more than on such occasions when the communication of their instant, even instantaneous thoughts and feelings blends them into the same rush of experience and sensation. George at times has his fill of it; the city for him is more to be conquered than savored. But Mrs. Jack can never get enough: "She loved the unending crowds. . . . The city was her garden of delight, her magic island, in which always she could find some new joy, some new rich picture to feed her memory."

Mrs. Jack is also a great giver of parties, attended by many of her celebrity friends. As a convenience to her urban-mad lover, she introduces him to both of Manhattan's geographic spreads. When they first meet, she lives in a house on the West Side. After he has taken this in thoroughly, she moves to an apartment on Park Avenue where he thrashes about with hostile eagerness in the affluent surroundings of one of the world's most famous neighborhoods. Her parties are a showcase of the city, plainly designed to give George a quick opportunity to meet writers, bankers, business executives, publishers, lawyers, men and women from the representative arts, and an assortment of "interesting" personalities.

George, naturally, wants to get his novel published and become famous himself in the city which is the center and creator of fame. Wolfe's own intention is somewhat different: he wants to master the city as a phenomenon of life, and he quite ruthlessly uses George and Mrs. Jack to this end. He is only marginally interested in George's ambition and exploits that ambition for his own purpose, conceiving the love affair as a chance to get at the city, where the affair begins and flourishes, and where it finally expires in pain and tumult.

When the lovers are alone, when the city fades from view and they are in their own private space, it is not the love act but the love emotion that is at the core of their relationship. Sex is indeed curiously absent or reduced to a minor role. They are two people in love, rather than two people loving or making love. Their feelings for each other are expressed far more eloquently and certainly at far greater length even in the meals they eat than in any consummated passion made visible to us. Dinner, which Mrs. Jack prepares joyously and skillfully, is an amorous ritual in the best erotic tradition of Rabelais and Fielding. The act of eating is less a preliminary to the act of love than a metaphorical substitute for it, with the table rather than the bed as the focal point. Their joy in eating, like the joy they find in talking with one another and being in one another's company, is dwelt on more lingeringly and makes a much more lasting impression upon us than their physical union, a union which, it is suggested, takes place often but which is alluded to in only the vaguest terms.

Food is in any case a subject sure to arouse Wolfe at any time. He never recovered from the epic repasts served by his father, and the poetry of eating well—which to him meant not just eating good food but eating it in gargantuan quantities—appears in his writing from the start and recurs throughout. It would not be extravagant to say that Wolfe is the greatest exponent of and certainly the greatest ecstasizer on food in American literature. Not even Hemingway, another aficionado among trenchermen, devotes as much energy to it or treats it with as much artistry.

Neither George nor Mrs. Jack is in control of their feelings. He is given to irrational outbursts during which, while claiming to love her, he deluges her with torrents of abuse—berating her for being Jewish; for being older than himself, old enough to be his mother; for patronizing him and thus gratifying herself with the vanity of "discovering" and "bringing" him along; for having a husband and children whom she has no intention of giving up for his sake; for wanting to possess, dominate, and smother him.

On her side, in a quite different tone, with a good deal of wit that does not conceal her underlying anxiety, she mocks his pretensions, derides his conceit, scorns his anti-Semitism, and wishes him a life of tasteless meals served badly by a dried-up, meager Christian girl. Most of the time she does not openly express such thoughts, though they go on at length in her mind. Only under extreme provocation, when he has taunted her beyond endurance, do they burst forth. He of course never holds back anything. With George, to feel is to speak.

In love, Wolfe's heroes express themselves verbally rather than sexually. In standard Freudian terms, they, like Wolfe himself, are highly developed oral types. They eat and they talk. The mouth is their primary organ and certainly their most highly developed one. It takes in impressions, sensations, food and drink, and emits feelings and the raw material of art. Though Wolfe labored hard over his books and revised them extensively, they still sound like oral gushings and outpourings which, almost accidentally, happen to have been set down on paper.

The sense of freshness and improvisation this conveys is immeasurable. Southerners, the country's natural orators, have produced in Wolfe one of literature's great natural orators, and it is this irresistible flow of verbal fluency and energy, coming from some inexhaustible source within, that is one of his most arresting and distinguishing qualities. The mouth is the supreme conduit of his existence as man and artist.

Mrs. Jack conducts George not only through the urban space which she occupies so comfortably but through urban time. Her father had been a prominent actor and figure about town back in the nineties, supplying her childhood with the splash and glitter that emanated from New York during one of its brilliant periods. A true creature of Wolfe's imagination, she is endowed with his fervent, hyperactive memory which seems to have retained the subtlest vibrations of the past. She proceeds to pour out all her recollections to George's outstretched ears.

Never was there a more willing and attentive audience. He drinks in, listens, and hangs on to her every word, asks the most searching questions about the tiniest minutiae, as though what he is hearing is not only manna for his soul but the gruel of life itself. He feels invigorated and in some profound way replenished by her outpourings. They are to work their way into his books and thus nourish his career as an artist. They also supply him with a rich source of accumulated human energy, the energy of her life going back to its origins. He is Mrs. Jack's lover, but he is also her researcher, pursuing to the last footnote the supreme object of his research, herself, and through her the life-span of the great city which, past and present, she embodies. Seldom in literature has there been so complete a transfer of a human table of contents from one person to another.

When this transfer, in both space and time, is complete, George is ready to break off from Mrs. Jack. He finds her no less attractive than ever. There has been no diminution in her warmth or vitality, and certainly none in her attention to his wants. But since he is not primarily interested in her as a woman, a mistress, or a cook, her unchanged condition along these lines is of no avail.

The reason he gives himself for ending their relationship is that she is too possessive, that he feels increasingly dominated and owned by her, and must assert his own independence. But this is contrary to the obvious facts of their case. She is in truth far more emotionally dependent on him than he on her. The services she performs for him, the introductions she provides, earn her as much abuse from him as gratitude. His real reason for rejecting her, underlying the rationalized one, a reason that as a character in the book he is only vaguely aware of, is that she is of no further use to him as a guide to the world, and particularly to the world of the city. In this he discharges once again his supreme function as agent of the author. As man and lover, George has had no change of heart. As Wolfe's urban researcher, however, his project, as it were, has come to an end.

When it is over, he bids farewell to Mrs. Jack and takes off for Germany where we see him, in the final chapter, convalescing in a Munich hospital from a brawl at the Munich fair and, with his bruised face staring at itself in a mirror, engaged in a lively debate between his body and soul. For the historical record, the debate ends in a draw.

When Wolfe, in the Author's Note to *The Web and the Rock*, declares it to be his most objective novel, he is of course defying the critics who had accused him of being able to write only about himself. But he is doing more than that. He is announcing an intention that goes far beyond the immediate question of "subjective" and "objective," of whether he can create characters instead of just copying them down, of whether he is doomed by some fatal defect of the imagination to the confining facts of his own biography.

That intention is to move from the particular to the general, from the immediate to the permanent, from this moment in time and this point in space to the representation of time and space themselves. So in George's love affair with Mrs. Jack, it is the emotion he is after, not the act; it is less their individual feelings for one another than the feeling of being in love, the element commonly present in love experienced by all men and women. If such a common element can be said to exist, that is what Wolfe is after.

He seeks to rescue feeling and sensation from the transient flux in which they live so vividly and briefly by seizing their enduring qualities, the qualities that are there whenever particular feelings and sensations appear and reappear in the endless occasions of the here and now. He is not primarily a describer or creator of men and women but a searcher after mankind. He is in fact no longer a writer of novels but a universal scene painter, and the needs of storytelling—credibility, orderliness, disciplined form—have been outrightly subordinated, if not actually submerged, to the needs of getting at humanity in the largest sense, in the sense of being alive inside the encompassing frame of the universe. One cannot get more "objective" than this. No writer who ever lived had a more "objective" object in view.

We have said that, among his contemporaries, the later Wolfe most closely resembles Dos Passos, in intention though not in texture or sensory detail. As he moves away from the grooves of familiar fiction—whether it be the experimental fiction of Joyce, whom he so consciously imitated in *Look Homeward, Angel,* or the traditional narrative of classic novelists like Henry Fielding and George Eliot—he begins to resemble, among the figures of the past, mutational novelists like Rabelais and Swift. Mutational in that neither was, strictly speaking, a novelist at all. Rabelais was a doctor who, aroused by the follies and depravities of his time, created the adventures of Gargantua and Pantagruel as a club to attack the corruptions of the day.

Swift was a parson equally incensed at human irrationality and folly, who wrote *Gulliver's Travels* as a mirror in which men could see themselves precisely reflected. It was Swift's hope that this might result in a reformation of their ways, though it was his gloomy and despairing conviction that mankind was probably beyond remedy. *Gulliver's Travels,* like the books of Rabelais, bears a surface resemblance to a novel, in places reads like one, yet it is not exactly a novel, and in the end is not one at all. Wolfe's later books move erratically yet powerfully in this general direction. *The Web and the Rock* is a distinctly clearer example of this movement than *Of Time and the River. You Can't Go Home Again* will be the clearest example yet.

Rabelais and Swift were both satirists. They used highly inventive forms of exaggeration to pump up their targets in order to make them as dramatically visible as possible. In the last paragraph of his Author's Note, Wolfe informs us that *The Web and the Rock* "has in it, from first to last, a strong element of satiric exaggeration: not only because it belongs to the nature of the story . . . but because satiric exaggeration also belongs to the nature of life, and particularly American life."

Exaggeration came naturally to Wolfe. He absorbed it from the tall tales native to the mountain region where he grew up. Southern speechmaking, dinned into his ears as a boy, was rich, ornate, and full of hyperbole—Southern oratory was almost the last bastion of the baroque. Some of it came from his family, devoted as they were, young and old alike, to the unrestrained emotional life. It came also from the special circumstance of his being outsized, which meant a constant straining—as he poignantly describes in the short story "Gulliver"—either to shrink himself to the proportions of others or inflate them to match his own. The tendency to magnify is in his work from the start, as it was in his nature. Even a casual reading reveals dozens of instances, from the emotional outpourings and temperamental violence of his heroes to the vast sweeps over continental and planetary landscapes.

Less obvious but just as significant is his tendency to miniaturize, to reduce a large subject to single examples, and by concentrating on a single example, force it to yield the secrets of the whole to which it is attached. Both techniques are essential in satire, as Swift illustrated in his celebrated work. He applies reduction in Lilliput and magnification in Brobdingnag. In *The Web and the Rock*, Wolfe applies reduction in North Carolina and, for the most part, magnification in New York.

When Wolfe wishes to pinpoint time, he composes a

54-page chapter on three o'clock. When he deals with race relations, yet wants to avoid an essay on the subject, he reveals in the explosive episode of Dick Prosser the swing from servility to violence that marks the intimate connection between black and white. When he tries to get at beauty, it is not the Taj Mahal, the Isles of Greece, or Keats that he dwells on but "a spur of rusty boxcars on a siding, curving off somewhere into a flat of barren pine and clay." He gets at the idea of love by the sight of Mrs. Jack, delicately flushed, bending over the stove as she cooks dinner. And he manages to find in a melon or a roast of beef all the juiciness linked with sex.

Wolfe can take some small object, and work it over until it yields up its revelation, with the same élan with which he swoops over a mountain range or puffs up an emotion until it fills the world. He has his circuits of energy that magnetize him, with roughly equal frequency, in the directions of large and small. The cliché about his gigantism, his relentless impulse to inflate, must be corrected in the light of the countermovement in him to reduce, to deflate, and, keeping in mind the general proportion of his work, to concentrate on the head of a pin.

The ratio of impersonal to personal material is much greater in *The Web and the Rock* than in *Of Time and the River,* when the change in Wolfe visibly began. His third novel is devoted to two large subjects—the Southern town and the Northern city. It starts off with George Webber's boyhood in North Carolina which, in drastic contrast to Eugene's boyhood in the same area, is concerned not with the developing ego of the boy but with the ambience of the region. In fact, George as a boy is almost invisible. He does not emerge as himself. Wolfe deliberately keeps him under wraps so that he may more conveniently and detachedly play the role of observer.

Even observer is too strong a term. Focus would perhaps be more accurate. He is a focus or funnel through which Wolfe can conduct his real business, which is not to show the growth of a personality but to draw a graphic, highly impressionistic, terrifically energized portrait of the South. And in this portrait, like so many chunky tidbits in a fruitcake, there is scattered decisive information about Southern landscape, weather, Negroes, violence, football and football heroes, college life, provincial patriotism, and reverence for war as one of the supreme human experiences.

In New York, George does emerge. Not all at once and certainly not at first. At first he is only one of a cluster of young Southerners who room together and roam about the city sharing more or less the same initial impressions, go out with girls, horse around, attend the Dempsey-Firpo fight, get tired of each other, quarrel, break up, and finally go their separate ways. Even when George begins teaching at the School of Utility Cultures, he remains nebulous—he issues a succession of sneers at the school but is never seen in the classroom. It is not until he is introduced to us as a writer and then meets Mrs. Jack that he becomes manifest for the first time as himself.

Unlike Eugene, his predecessor along the track of romantic youth, George's personality is only minimally developed. It seems to consist of only two impulses: a strain of mad violence inherited from his mother's family and a passion for order and discipline attributed to his father. "Two Worlds Discrete," one of the book's section titles, is Wolfe's description of this duality. Discrete is just the word for it: the two impulses are not only totally separate from one another but appear to be mutually exclusive. George experiences them one at a time, never both at once. At any given moment he is a simple or simplified organism. Wolfe's intention to present him that way is made evident when, as a child, George is abruptly severed from both his parents. His father goes off and his mother dies, so that we are never allowed to see him, as we do Eugene, growing up in the thick generative soil of a living family.

George is thus detached from the complexities of a fully realized character while continuing to give off its heat and energy. But the very element that makes him less convincing than Eugene on human grounds is what makes him the more useful to Wolfe as the agent of his new intentions. George has plenty of temperament but very little personality. He has a strong capacity to feel and react but no marked traits or even quirks of character. Psychologically he is fixed rather than mobile, and can be counted on to respond in much the same way to whatever he is involved in.

This is a great aid to Wolfe. He does not have to worry about his hero developing a streak of independence, becoming balky or recalcitrant, acquiring an autonomous existence, or refusing to obey his author's instructions. He is a perfect example of what E. M. Forster called a flat rather than a round character: i.e., a character whose attitude is predictable and who never surprises us by behaving unexpectedly. Wolfe has programmed him for another purpose: to move from personality to process, from fact to feeling, from action to emotion, from being the center of a particular story to being the catalyst of what lies beyond it, the catalyst of its permanent and recurring qualities that do not depend on immediate circumstance.

Like Plato, Wolfe wants to get at the essence of things. But unlike Plato, he does not want to transcend sense or escape time. He wants instead to root his essences in the loam of sense impressions, like a tree that can ascend toward heaven only because it is firmly planted in the earth. And far from longing to escape from time into the timeless, he wants to control time by forcing it to stand still. He emphatically does not want to get beyond it into Plato's firmament of ideas and disembodied thought.

It is tremendously important to him as an imaginative writer intensely attracted to the sensuous that time go on, for only the flow of ongoing time creates the new material and the new experience so vitally necessary to his imagination. But the act of memory that makes time stop is equally essential, and to this act Wolfe bends all his energies, straining, almost compelling the past by a supreme effort of the will to reappear in his mind with absolute fidelity. Eugene and George both go through agonies of recall, bellowing out their hunger to recapture everything, and by recapturing it create it all over again.

If the original experience is life, the re-created one is art, and Wolfe is fascinated by both in about equal measure. He wants to live and he also wants to write, gradually working himself to the point where the two become indistinguishable. Toward the end, it is not enough for him to live through an experience; it will not seem complete until he writes about it as well. When that happens, as it does in the later novels, the gap between George Webber experiencing something and cramming it into his book all but disappears. By the time we get to *You Can't Go Home Again*, he has been turned into a pure instrument of recall and re-creation.

The personal, biographical element is still present, though severely restrained, in the early stages of *The Web and the*

Rock. This grows steadily more tenuous as Wolfe gets into the New York phase of the novel. Though George's affair with Mrs. Jack is marked by frenzied outbursts of temperament, these are only a gloss on his determined exploitation of her in pursuit of Wolfe's search for the soul of the city. The two lovers work out their love relationship at considerable length, but from the outset Wolfe is looking beyond them at the enfabled rock which he seeks to scale. Even to his seething ambition, this enterprise appears Himalayan in scope, a prospect that might discourage the rest of us but that only stimulates him to plunge ahead. It is this plunging ahead, past the characters and their particular lives, that carries Wolfe far beyond the familiar limits and conventional format of *Look Homeward, Angel.*

Read as a traditional novel, *The Web and the Rock* suffers by comparison with the earlier book. Read, as I believe it should be, as an intensely articulated mural, first of the provincial and then, climactically, of the urban landscape, it not only does not suffer by comparison with its famous predecessor, but is not to be compared with it at all.

It is in a category by itself. Taken on its own terms, *The Web and the Rock* is an extraordinarily interesting and highly original example of a work breaking out of the confines of its own genre. It is a triumph of Wolfe's newly directed art, another stage in the saga of a novelist getting away from the novel.

5

You Can't Go Home Again

The title of Wolfe's fourth novel is unexpectedly prophetic. He meant of course that you can't go back to your early youth, to your hometown, to the way things were. But in a sense the title also applies to the movement of his art. It, too, cannot return to its starting point. Once it alters course, it moves irresistibly away from its own origins. With the advent of *You Can't Go Home Again,* Wolfe's first novel, *Look Homeward, Angel,* which had grown visibly more remote on the general landscape of his writing, now vanishes altogether as a point of reference.

The tone of this final book is drier than usual, the writing more cramped. The subject matter is aggressively sociological, at times grimly so. The two great experiences of the 1930s—the depression and the rise of the Fascist empires— are more vividly present than were earlier contemporary events in the preceding novels. The explosive release of energy that followed the First World War and carried through the 1920s was now checked, turned away from rampant, freewheeling individualism to the collective actions of the following decade. Even Wolfe's torrential outpouring was at last slowed down. Even his headlong Faustian assault on the universe was reined in. *You Can't Go Home Again* is the tribute wrung from Wolfe by the times. It is his version of the depression novel.

It opens in the summer of 1929, a fateful season as the country—and the world—lurch blindly toward the darkness ahead. George is back from his European trip, much chastened. He has learned his lesson: You can't eat your cake and have it, too, Wolfe asserts; one can't devour the earth; reason and emotion must pull together. And similar banalities. They may all be true, but one wishes that Wolfe had found fresher ways of putting them.

Still, George's "frenzy" seems curbed, and as a sign of his new maturity, he resumes his relationship with Mrs. Jack, only this time in an apartment of his own, a marked departure from the quarters jointly rented and shared at the beginning of their affair. While the country is on the verge of the stock-market crash, George is on the verge of getting his first book published, so that the story begins at a moment of impending climax, with tremendous things in the offing.

The first three chapters are written in a pleasant, engaging, and for Wolfe, quiet tone, in pointed contrast with his more publicized style of feverish grandiosity. But though dealing with personal matters and arrangements, it is all strikingly impersonal. Hardly anything further is said about George's connection with Mrs. Jack and nothing at all about the novel that is about to make him famous. Instead we are regaled with a vignette of an eccentric Japanese sculptor who lives

downstairs and with Manhattan street scenes largely involving trucks.

Wolfe is as enthusiastic about trucks as he is about trains
and ocean liners, and truck drivers qualify, along with
locomotive engineers, policemen, lumberjacks, and prize
fighters, as embodiments, in his view, of manliness, strength,
and purity of soul. The manuscript of his now-accepted novel
gives George entrée to publishing circles, and he presents us
with detailed sketches of editors and publishers, culminating
in the appearance of Foxhall Edwards, universally acknowl-
edged to be Maxwell Perkins himself.

There is throughout these early pages a determined and
successful attempt at detachment, at placing maximum
distance between the observer and the observed.

The death of his aunt summons George home to the South,
and he boards car K 19 for the 700-mile journey from New
York to Libya Hill. This train ride is a deliberate and
instructive reversal of Eugene's celebrated journey by train in
exactly the opposite direction in *Of Time and the River*.
Nothing here about the landscape, none of those vast sweeps
over America, by both night and day, to which Eugene's
soaring imagination drove him and that the rush of the train
through space made so appropriate. Instead we get what
amounts to a social study of a middling-sized Southern
town—the original Asheville, no doubt, but altered somewhat in its fictional transformations first to Altamont and now
to Libya Hill.

On K 19, George runs into three fellow townsmen sharing
the same trip back, chosen apparently because each stands
for something large and significant in the life of the town.
One is the mayor, a hearty, glad-handing, municipal booster
straight out of *Babbitt*. The second is Judge Bland, an

embittered old lawyer, now blind, who has made his living
lending money to impoverished Negroes at usurious rates of
interest and, like an aging, self-hating Tiresias, prophesies
doom for the money-greedy town. The third is Nebraska
Crane, the major-league baseball star, going home briefly in
mid-season to recover from a leg injury.

Like George Willard, everybody's confidant in *Winesburg,
Ohio*, George Webber "interviews" these three representative figures, which means that he sits around listening to them
tell their tales; in the process, they lay out the social structure
of Libya Hill: the mayor with his bluff, fatuous optimism;
Judge Bland, corrupted himself and therefore an acknowl-
edged expert on the corruption of the community; and
Crane, innocent in spirit and pure of heart, who looks upon
home as a place to live in and plant roots in, who repudiates
land-greedy real-estate speculation and the malignant fever
of the boom. By the time K 19 reaches its destination, we are
already supplied with a fundamental blueprint of the American town swollen with the bloat of prosperity and on the
slippery edge of collapse.

In 1936, Robert and Helen Lynd had published *Middletown*, their celebrated profile of Muncie, Indiana. Zeroing in
on towns and cities—as though the pathology of a nation
could best be exposed through the small end of the telescope
—was a favorite approach of the thirties. Wolfe, too, is
caught up in the fervor of the historical moment and moves
toward socioeconomic matters that would have been incon-
ceivable in the time of Eugene Gant.

George attends the funeral of his aunt, renews old
acquaintances, enjoys the stir of interest at the news that his
novel will soon appear. His return home winds up with three
successive chapters whose titles suggest the vein of social

consciousness opening out and spreading in Wolfe. Chapter 7, "Boom Town," describes the crowded streets of Libya Hill, the populace convulsed with the fever to make quick killings in real estate. Chapter 8, "The Company," recounts the melancholy story of George's friend, Randy Shepperton, exploited and then fired by the company to which he had given years of faithful service. Chapter 9, "The City of Lost Men," is Wolfe's jeremiad against the money hunger that has carried America away from its original destiny. George has gone to the cemetery to place flowers on his aunt's grave. There, at dusk, looking down from "the great hill of the dead" at the town whose lights are now coming on one by one, he savagely predicts the catastrophe ahead and the coming darkness, knowing with painful certitude, as he leaves for New York, that he, like the country, can't go home again.

The Manhattan landscape is now seen through the same sociological keyhole as Libya Hill's. In a series of animated portraits, the lives of the wealthy—which in New York meant the liberal-minded wealthy—are sketched in as symbolic illustrations of the city as society. The moment is still October 1929, with the great city of the North, like the small city of the South, on the edge of collapse. At this point Wolfe shoulders George aside and, ruthlessly intervening as the omniscient author, does the whole job himself.

He begins with Mr. Jack, who makes his first appearance onstage after having hovered vaguely in the wings throughout almost the whole of his wife's love affair with George Webber. "Jack at Morn" is the title of the chapter which shows him waking up in his Park Avenue apartment, drifting through a series of early-morning sensations and thoughts, pushing himself through a series of calisthenics, and stepping into his bath. While all this is going on, Wolfe follows him about as an invisible presence, taking everything down in a journalistic shorthand quite as though he were on assignment from *The New Yorker* or *Esquire*. Mr. Jack is perfectly turned out—a sleek, hard, smoothly tailored urban missile: "His tallowy flesh seemed to have been compacted . . . out of a common city-substance—the universal grey stuff of pavements, buildings, towers, tunnels, and bridges. In his veins there seemed to flow and throb, instead of blood, the crackling electric current by which the whole city moved."

His appearance, solo at first, is paired at breakfast with Mrs. Jack's. They quarrel amiably; their domestic tensions have no sexual content. He goes off to Wall Street in his chauffeured limousine, and she engages in an unpleasant hassle with her maid over the theft of a dress. Nothing is resolved, leaving both sides fretful. In Wolfe's version, the collapse of America is prefaced by the dissolution of ties between the upper and lower classes. Traditional harmony between master and servant is unraveling. Presently our inquiring reporter descends in the same apartment house to the elevator operators, doormen, and swampers—the working class, quarreling among themselves over such matters as joining the union. Tension between classes is accompanied by discord within them. Wolfe works his way both vertically and laterally on the social scale.

Mrs. Jack is preparing a great party, one of the glittering affairs of the season to which she is inviting her celebrity friends and wringing from George his reluctant agreement to attend. The setting is grand, even grandiose. The party itself is described in elaborate detail, an intricate kaleidoscope of food, drink, and conversation, with entertainment provided by a popular, fashionable puppeteer and clown whose appeal is flagrantly lascivious, sly, and decadent. Occurring as it does on the eve of the great crash, it vaguely recalls Pompeii and Herculaneum glistening with luxury as Vesuvius erupts, the Roman Empire as the Huns arrive, Marie Antoinette turning on all the lights at Versailles as the Bastille is being stormed, the Czar wonderfully unconscious of anything untoward, with the Bolsheviks gathering in the wings.

Wolfe's historical and sociological intentions are clear, perhaps too much so. A fire breaks out in the apartment house in the middle of the party. Everyone rushes out to the street, and in the chill darkness are obscurely conscious that something has changed. Something indeed has. The old order is over, while the face of the new is not yet visible in the looming chaos.

The fire is an advance agent of the imminent crash, a warning of what is ahead. Two men working in the house are trapped in an elevator and are suffocated by smoke. Premonitions of disaster are everywhere, in the presence of the police, ambulances, the interrupted party, the human expulsion from light to darkness, all taking place on the richest street of the richest city of the richest country in the world. George scarcely has to draw the necessary conclusion for us: that America can't go home, that a return to the old ways is no longer possible. In such assertions, Wolfe links the personal situation of his hero with regard to Libya Hill with the corresponding situation of the country, and thus heralds George's arrival into a state of full social consciousness.

The break with the past is the signal for George to break off with Mrs. Jack, this time for good. The crash immediately follows, burying the old America under its debris. Its effects, visible enough in Manhattan, are catastrophic in Libya Hill where the real-estate boom collapses with shattering force. Among its coincidental disasters is the hostile furor aroused by George's book, much like Asheville's bitter reading of *Look Homeward, Angel.* This bruises the author, and the pain is not quite soothed by his literary success in New York, where he enjoys for a time the heady tonic of being a young lion. Not for long, however. As part of his newly acquired sense of how the rich exploit the poor, George feels himself exploited as a celebrity by rich women, rich hostesses, and hungry climbers who pursue and try to use him for their own purposes. He resolves to free himself of Manhattan, of its rich and fashionable world, of Mrs. Jack and everything she represents. To escape, he retreats across the river to Brooklyn.

At this point, a little past its halfway mark, the design of Wolfe's final book is clear, and stands in a line of logical progression with the earlier works. The main arena of *Look Homeward, Angel* was the internal consciousness. *Of Time and the River* and *The Web and the Rock* swerve—indeed leap—from there to explorations of the outer world conceived in the widest and farthest terms. Now, in this fourth production, Wolfe takes hold of what lies between the individual and the world itself, the structure and operations of society.

True to his later form, his "social" scenes have little to do with fiction. They do not advance the story or reveal the characters, except insofar as they deal with a historical situation to which everyone is reacting in much the same way. It is pure sociohistory, concealed—but with less and less effort at concealment—inside the format of a novel. Much of it may seem to us clumsy and heavy-handed, with its symbolism all too obvious. Yet it is profoundly faithful to that ultimate movement of Wolfe's imagination working its way through the conditions of men to reach, if possible, the state of man.

He is always struggling to arrive at what, for him, are fresh perceptions. In the first half of *You Can't Go Home Again* he is preoccupied with the rich. He comes to see very clearly and to represent effectively that, of the two kinds of rich, each is equally responsible for the plight of the country. The crude, cutthroat, robber-baron rich need no further identification. But the liberal rich, for all their attractive manners and advanced ideas, for all their professed sympathies with the downtrodden, live off the misery, poverty, and sweated labor of the masses quite as much as do the straight-out, no-nonsense exploiters. This is George's conclusion about Mrs. Jack and her liberal-minded crowd. Their hypocrisy, however unconscious, finally severs the link between them, and prepares the way for the aggressive humanitarianism that is to grow in George during the depression years in the depths of Brooklyn.

The Brooklyn chapters initiate Wolfe's preoccupation with the victims of society—the masses who are the victims of the depression, the Jews who are the victims of the Nazis, and even the artist who is in a sense the victim of life, who bears upon his shoulders the weight of living, the burden of his perceptions, who even if he succeeds, like Sinclair Lewis (appearing in the book under the name of Lloyd McHarg), does so only at the price of life exhaustion.

In its swing through sociology and contemporary history, *You Can't Go Home Again* divides naturally into two parts, its earlier sections an inquiry into the upper social level, its later ones into the lower. The book acquires its shape not through the psychological changes of a novel but through the logical format of a tract. It is Wolfe's tract for the times.

The facts of George's life in Brooklyn are tailored to suit the historical occasion. The dark basement in which he lives and writes is more like a dungeon than a room, its two small windows high up in the wall braced with iron bars. It is flanked by "the shacks, tenements, and slums in all the raw rusty streets and alleys of South Brooklyn" and pervaded by the stink of the Gowanus Canal. "He has come here deliberately, driven by a resolution to seek out the most forlorn and isolated hiding spot that he could find." If the mass of his compatriots are to live in squalor, so will he. Everything he does is now heavily instinct with social consciousness, so that the very words used to describe his years in Brooklyn are perfectly applicable to America in the early thirties:

> They were hard years, desperate years, lonely years, years of interminable writing and experimentation, years of exploration and discovery, years of grey timelessness, weariness, exhaustion, and self-doubt.

When he is not writing, he prowls the streets, crosses the Brooklyn Bridge on foot into lower Manhattan, and in the shadow of the great buildings and banks of Wall Street describes with bitter, brilliant candor the masses of unemployed men huddling for shelter in the latrines and platforms of the subway. The details and arrangements here are much as they were in the cartoons of the *New Masses*, the ballads of Woody Guthrie, and the pages of the most celebrated of the depression novels, *The Grapes of Wrath*: symbols of wealth and poverty side by side, the one heartless and immoral, the other suffering and blameless. Wolfe does not go beyond this crude juxtaposition of vice and virtue, but the searing energy with which he catches the human scene during this depressed historical moment lights up his own newly acquired awareness of what is going on in the immediate world around him.

During his endless walks, George scornfully observes the coming-out party of a rich debutante. He comments in mourning accents on the emptiness of city youth, "Those straggling bands of boys of sixteen or eighteen . . . going along a street, filling the air with raucous jargon and senseless cries . . . with joyless catcalls and mirthless quips and jokes. . . . Where here, among these lads, is all the merriment, high spirits, and spontaneous gayety of youth?" And he records with surprise the persistent optimism of the Americans; amid their misery and hopelessness, they continue to believe that something is bound to turn up. This paradox fills him with wonder and admiration, touches him profoundly, and re-awakens in him even during periods of extreme melancholy a tenderness for America.

His feelings are climaxed by the four remarkable pages that bring Chapter 27 to its Shakespearean finale. Beginning with the question, "For what is man?", Wolfe takes off like a verbal rocket through the several stages of human life, through the greatness and meanness of human nature, and winds up in a flurry of approbation of man's instinct for life and resistance to death.

In Wolfe's pictorial art, there is seldom room for more than one figure at a time. George now disappears once again and is replaced this time by Foxhall Edwards, his editor. Like Uncle Bascom, Dick Prosser, and Mr. Jack, his portrait is highly stylized and fills the canvas to the farthest corner. Like them, Edwards is not a fully developed individual with an assemblage of traits and feelings. He is, instead, a collection of eccentricities held together by an animating principle of mind. His determining gesture is a persistent sniff; he wears hats in restaurants; he gives outrageous tips for obscure reasons; he is astringently ironic with his numerous daughters.

Behind his eccentricities is his essential view of things: aristocratic, selective, profoundly conservative, scornful of the empty rich but refusing to be sentimental about the poor, believing that life is a tragedy that cannot be changed, yet believing also in hard work and the splendor of personal example. He has exactly the kind of mind that George—and Wolfe—tremendously admire and are to have a tremendous quarrel with in the last two chapters of the book.

At breakfast one morning Fox's eye falls on a small newspaper item about a man named C. Green who jumped out of a window in the Admiral Drake Hotel in Brooklyn and fell to his death. He sniffs and instantly reconstructs the whole story of this anonymous and obscure suicide. Using C. Green as an exemplar of an average American, Wolfe launches into a 25-page sociological journey through America, this time on the level of the lower middle class. C. Green's life—and certainly his death—may not have been consequential in the light of eternity or even the eye of history. But as a microcosm of middle-class America, he is of immense value to Wolfe, working his sociological field.

While bemoaning the misery of the masses, Wolfe never loses sight for long of the misery of the artist. The critics, aesthetes, apes of fashion, schools of advanced thought, who irritated George in *The Web and the Rock* while he was living in Manhattan, now follow him across the river to Brooklyn, extracting from him fresh explosions of satirical rage.

He attacks the magazines: "We have allowed ourselves to

be bored, maddened . . . hound-and-hornered, nationed, new-republicked, dialed, spectatored, mercuried, storied, anviled, new-massed, new-yorkered, vogued, vanity-faired, timed, broomed, transitioned . . . by the . . . Blotters of the Arts." And the individual critics, whom he seeks to demolish with ridicule: "Your little seldesey-weldesey, cowley-wowley, tatesy-watesy, hicksy-picksy, wilsony-pilsony, jolasy-wolasy, steiny-weiny, goldy-woldly, sneer-puss fellows. . . . Your groupy-croupy, cliquey-triquey, meachy-teachy devoto-bloato wire-pullers and back-scratchers of the world."

The idea of the artist as victim of the world's cruelty, malice, and exploitation fits in comfortably with Wolfe's aroused social conscience. George Webber, roaming through the debris of the depression in the streets of the great city, feels spiritually at home. He, too, is after all one of the system's natural targets.

But clearly not a passive one. He lashes back at his tormentors, refuses to accept the status quo as part of an inevitable order of things, and continues to believe fervidly in his own recuperative powers. He links these with the recuperative powers of the country. In a superb passage that highlights Chapter 31, Wolfe launches into another of his soaring declamations about the resurgent energies of America. The passage, playing with great virtuosity on the refrain "Burning in the night," brings the Brooklyn years to an end and ushers in the final phases of the book.

Having finished his second novel, George takes off for Europe, carrying Wolfe's sociology with him. In England he devotes himself to an extended essay on the social opinions and political attitudes of his cleaning woman, Daisy Purvis. Despite her lowly standing in class terms, she is more Tory than the Tories, and George shrewdly records her prejudices, bigotries, and convictions with the skill of a professional reporter. Mrs. Purvis and her world are scarcely new phenomena, but Wolfe handles this standard figure with great vitality and considerable humor.

In England, too, George has a fascinating encounter with Lloyd McHarg, the famous American novelist and Nobel Prize winner, now at the height of his fame. McHarg is a ravaged victim of his own success. He drove himself to achieve it, and is exhausting himself retaining it. The demands made upon him in the writing of his books, in acting out the role of a celebrity, in being thrust into a level of intense experience where he is under unrelenting pressure from the world and from his own sense of himself, have drained him of his life energies and brought him to the edge of collapse. Not from any physical ailment but through a kind of psychic attrition, a persisting spiritual hemorrhage which is now too far advanced to be sealed off. He is as much the target of the world's oppression as the unemployed worker brought down by hard times. From Wolfe's viewpoint, the artist is the martyr of experience, and never more so than when he appears most triumphant.

After England comes a final, climactic visit to Germany. It is the summer of 1936. The Nazis, flushed with their early power, are hosts to the Olympic Games and feel themselves to be the center of the world. So does George. He, too, is in the flush of early fame, and nowhere more so than in Germany where his books are devoured with admiration and he is a sort of junior Lloyd McHarg. "Life took on an added radiance. . . . because Fame was at his side. . . . It seemed to him that he had won a final and utterly triumphant victory over all the million forms of life. . . . He was life's strong and light-hearted master, and everyone he met . . . responded to

him eagerly . . . as men respond to the clean and shining
light of the young sun." The man and the country come
together here in one of those spectacular fusions that light up
the works of Wolfe with the swift unexpected flash of
summer lightning.

And vanish just as swiftly. For even George, insulated by
his own inflamed sense of success, cannot finally ignore what
is going on in Germany. He grows slowly, reluctantly aware
of the brutality, the police assaults, the barbarous treatment
of the Jews, and not just the Jews but all those at odds with
the regime. Gradually the malevolent atmosphere of the
Third Reich, corrupted and poisoned by the Nazis, seeps
through to him. "What George began to see was a picture of
a great people who had been psychically wounded and were
now desperately ill with some dread malady of the soul."

As the summer wears on, George feels increasingly split
between the royal treatment given him personally by the
Germans and the suppurating evidence of fear and persecu-
tion at every hand. On the train ride out of the country at the
end of his stay, he becomes friendly with the other passengers, including a German Jew trying to leave his native land.
He is seized at the border by the Gestapo. As he is being
taken away, he turns and gives the shocked passengers a final
look of anguish. "And in that gaze there was all the
unmeasured weight of man's mortal anguish. George and the
others felt somehow naked and ashamed. . . . they were
saying farewell, not to a man, but to humanity; not to some
pathetic stranger . . . but to mankind; not to some nameless
cipher out of life, but to the fading image of a brother's face."
As he leaves Germany, George knows it will be forever. This
country, to which he had been so deeply attached, which he
calls "the other part of his heart's home," joins the long list of

places and relationships that life has forced him to give up and to which he can never return.

Back in New York again, George proceeds to sever the last of his ties with the past, this time with his editor, the Foxhall Edwards of the book. He sends him a letter, an animated screed that covers thirty-five pages and brings *You Can't Go Home Again* to a close. It is a memoir, a confession, a credo, a spiritual autobiography, a highly dramatized philosophy of life, a last will and testament. It is Wolfe's summary of his own past and his highly charged vision of America as it is, as it ought to be, and in the light of Wolfe's eternally self-renewing optimism and affirmation, as it will be.

George admires Edwards as a generous and truly superior man but cannot stomach his conservative views. The conservative, like the Preacher in *Ecclesiastes*, believes that everything is vanity, that man's tragedy is that he must die, and it is therefore useless to try to improve the human lot. It can only be endured as best one can. George, with his newly acquired humanitarianism, will not tolerate this sense of futility. Everything the conservative says may rationally be true, but we must live as though it were wholly false. "Fear, hatred, slavery, cruelty, poverty, and need—can be conquered and destroyed. . . . but not by the tragic hypothesis that things as they are, evil as they are, are as good and as bad as, under any form, they will ever be."

Wolfe insists on the vital distinction between Eternity and Now. In the light of Eternity the conservative may be right. In the immediate Now, he is dead wrong, and Man-Alive, as Wolfe puts it, caught up in the growth and change of Now, can only devote himself to combating evil and advancing justice. If this is done—and it can be done only by overcoming the unyielding opposition of conservatives like Edwards—there is the blazing prospect of a new America, a new world, perhaps even a new mankind.

Wolfe now revives the metaphor of web and rock. Calling his editor a rock who stood by him during his most difficult hours, and himself a web or plant, George flashes over the whole of his life, going back to the beginning of things in the remote time of his ancestors. This final, almost apocalyptic sweep across time concludes with the remembered details of the sensory universe: the slamming of a gate, the smell of turnip greens, the clang of ice tongs, the blistered paint on the mantelpiece, "the casual stomping of a slow, gaunt hoof upon the pulpy lumber of a livery stable floor."

Having thus devoured the past and confronted the present, George is ready for the future. He has the sudden conviction —uncannily like the one that was soon to seize Wolfe when, mortally ill in a Seattle hospital, he sent a last foreboding note to Perkins that he will die. And even as he hears the wind rising, even as he feels the conscience of the world moving toward some as yet unseen horizon, he feels his own life approaching its close.

On this double note of cosmic exaltation and personal premonition, the last of Wolfe's titanic books comes to an end.

Comparing it with *Look Homeward, Angel*, one sees how far Wolfe has come in the journey of his art away from fiction, how much in his work the hero has been displaced by the subject. In that beginning book the writer's eye, and the reader's, are concentrated on Eugene almost without letup. Three volumes later the focus is almost everywhere but on

George. Eugene *was* the subject of his history. George is no longer the subject of his. His history is, in fact, part of a larger history and by no means its most essential part.

The writing current has been dramatically reversed. Instead of the world being absorbed into the protagonist, the protagonist moves outward into the world and for long stretches disappears in it. Wolfe ceases to be a student of character and becomes a craftsman of existence—existence in its multiple shapes, as sensation, as history, as landscape, as cosmos. What he learned from the writing of his one traditional novel was by no means lost; it is reflected in his later work as a muralist of universal forms.

An instructive view of Wolfe in his last stage can be gained by comparing *You Can't Go Home Again* with *The Grapes of Wrath*, another depression novel, perhaps the most famous example of its genre in the thirties. Both works were written in the last years of the decade and were published within a few months of each other. Both dealt with the social process and its victims. Both tended to moralize hard times by blaming misfortune on specific villains: the banks, the rich, the bosses, the Nazis; or on specific elements in human nature: cruelty, greed, the lust for power, and so on. Finally, both tended to see life in expanding terms: the Joads move from the family to the larger community of people like themselves to humanity at large, from the spirit of the Old Testament to the spirit of the New; George Webber moves from preoccupation with himself to concern and identification with the whole of mankind, a concern that is responsible for his break with Foxhall Edwards.

The two novels wonderfully reflect the two movements of the thirties: the contraction at the start and expansion at the end. One can say that Rose of Sharon offering her milky breast to the starving man on the last page of *The Grapes of Wrath* is a metaphor of the sentiments expressed in Wolfe's credo on the last pages of *You Can't Go Home Again*.

But their dissimilarities are equally striking. Steinbeck has a highly developed story line, pegged to that old, traditional, foolproof action, the journey. The problems, hardships, travails of the Joads during their odyssey to California and afterward generate a certain amount of suspense, draw the reader into a close relationship with them, and supply the novel with a substantial plot. Wolfe's book is plotless. It has no "story." It lacks a sequence of events that follow one another logically or causally. If the chapters on England and Germany were put in the middle of the book, for example, it would make no very great difference. A case could even be made for putting the letter to Edwards at the beginning and allowing the materials that follow to illustrate it.

Wolfe is concerned not with incidents that move forward but with situations that are fixed. They have an overall unity of their own: they deal with a period in history and express a particular frame of mind. But they are not locked into a narrative mold which requires a credible development from moment to moment. Like paintings dealing with a common theme, they can be hung on the wall any which way without essentially altering their impact.

Action in Steinbeck depends to some extent on character. Because Ma, Pa, Tom, Uncle John, Al, and the other Joads are the kind of people they individually are, they act in accordance with the demands of their personalities. Part of what happens to them results from disasters, both natural and man-made, beyond their control, but part is shaped by their private selves. There are just as many figures in Wolfe as in Steinbeck—George, Foxhall Edwards, Mrs. Jack, Mr. Jack,

Lloyd McHarg, Daisy Purvis (the London charwoman who serves as the instrument of George's inquiry into the British class system), and a host of minor personages—but they are not characters in a progressing narrative. They exist and function in themselves, as autonomous, self-sustaining units uninvolved with one another. The only thing they have in common is that they all know George; Wolfe can sketch them in against a flat rather than a moving background. Because of this, it is possible for him to finish their portraits.

Their portraits are finishable in a way that the characters in Steinbeck, forced by the story to be in a state of perpetual and uncertain change, cannot be finished or even rounded off. The result is that the products of Wolfe's imagination have a finality, an absoluteness lacking in the necessarily more fluid and temporal creatures of Steinbeck. What Steinbeck's people gain in dramatic tension, Wolfe's gain in psychological completeness and certainty. The point is not which is the better book or who the better writer, but that as books and writers they are profoundly different. Steinbeck is still operating within the confines of familiar fiction. Wolfe is not.

A final difference is the way in which they stretch their frames of reference. Every work of art seeks to generalize upon itself, to suggest that what it is dealing with is elemental in human experience and has repeatedly happened before, so that the immediate subject acquires a resonance that arises from all its previous appearances.

Steinbeck's way of tapping this resonance is to saturate *The Grapes of Wrath* with allusions to nothing less formidable and all-encompassing than the Bible. The Joads, like the Israelites, are fleeing from a region of disaster toward the promised land flowing with milk and honey. In their case the promised land is California, flowing with peaches and oranges. There are twelve Joads, as there were twelve Judean tribes. They move not just from Oklahoma to California but from the clannish spirit of the Old Testament to the universalized religion of the New. Tom Joad begins as Moses and ends as St. Paul. Steinbeck does not work all this in on a crude one-on-one basis, but his references are numerous and unmistakable. By tying his novel in with the most famous book in the world, he plainly hopes to make his story something more than a regional moment in the 1930s.

Wolfe's object is the same, but his approach is altogether different. His figures and scenes are not linked with any specific predecessors. They do not acquire their vitality from being like others but from what they suggest as themselves. They are generalized rather than particularized elements. Again, it is their representational rather than their individually shared character that Wolfe is getting at.

George Webber's erratic frenzies are not intended to remind us of similar outbursts by earlier artists; what emerges is their own special combination of energy, naïveté, and egomania. The smooth morning movements of Mr. Jack reveal a type of self-assured, self-satisfied businessman who is intended to embody the whole genre, yet he stands by himself, thoroughly detached, even disengaged from everything around him. Mrs. Jack, Lloyd McHarg, and the others are also individually self-contained figures seen less against the background of the particular book than within the framework of abstract reality.

The events of Wolfe's last work are equally self-sustaining. The depression and its painful consequences, the Nazis and their ghastly cruelties, are phenomena of so remarkable a kind that they remind us not of other such events but only and overwhelmingly of themselves. Wolfe achieves his effect by detaching his materials from their immediate contexts. He wants to save them from the homogenizing effect of time by forcing them to exist without connections. By compelling them to absolute independence, he imposes upon them the ultimate obligation to exist as themselves.

You Can't Go Home Again is a logical stage in Wolfe's continuing effort to develop an art that would release him, the products of his imagination, and even the overriding events of his own day from the restrictive categories of the traditional novel. He cut away its interconnective tissues, freeing his characters to stand on their own and exercise their own natures without interference. This simplified them; yet it exalted them, too.

Wolfe did not live long enough to perfect his new procedures, but his last three novels, and the last one in particular, are testimonials to the originality of his design and the tenacity with which he pursued it.

6

Two Stories

♈♈ Wolfe had a flair for short fiction as well as long: he turned out to be a very good and very skillful writer of short stories. He composed his own special brand of stories which depended less on plot than mood, less on action and incident than on perception and the feel of things. A fair number made their way into the novels. Two collections—one published while Wolfe was alive, the other posthumously— stand by themselves, and are reasonably representative of his efforts along these lines. They include some particularly well-known stories, like "Chickamauga" and "The Web of Earth," the one narrated by a returning veteran of the Confederate Army, the other by Eliza Gant in an extended recollection of her mountain ancestors. Both display Wolfe's underrated capacity to get out of himself and into the minds of others.

Instead of surveying everything in the two volumes, let us

concentrate on two especially splendid tales, one from each book. If Wolfe had written nothing else, these would have been enough to establish his genius and justify his standing among the formidable writers of his day.

The first of these, "In The Park," appeared in the earlier collection which came out in 1935, *From Death To Morning*. It is a reminiscence, apparently by Mrs. Jack, of her life as a young girl in New York at the turn of the century, and of one evening in particular at the beginning of May. She was eighteen, the year before her father died, and the coming of a radiant spring that year seemed to coincide with her own age, with the sense of New York bursting with opulence and energy, and her feeling for her father, an actor with a highly developed appetite for living.

After the evening performance of the play in which he is performing, he takes her to a Broadway restaurant where they eat, drink, and chatter amiably with a pair of stagestruck priests. Then they go for a ride in a horseless carriage to Central Park. They are stopped by a mounted policeman who scolds them for frightening his horse. The car breaks down. It mysteriously starts up again, and carries them triumphantly into the park where, under the glistening stars, they ride about all night. At dawn they hear the birds breaking into song, an eloquent finale to an ecstatic occasion. And on that note the story ends.

In terms of plot it could scarcely be lighter or thinner. It consists of some engaging chatter in a restaurant and a ride in the park. Neither the conversation nor the ride leads anywhere in particular; they have no visible aim aside from registering their own existence. Yet the story is a delicate masterpiece, revealing Wolfe's ability to work in a small frame—which was quite as much within his power as his better-known, more widely publicized ability to operate in a large expanse. What he is after is the sense of joy, of life at high tide, not because anything special is happening but as a thing in itself, generating its own radiance, a radiance to which the high-spirited young girl narrating the tale in the first person is responding with uncommon depth of feeling.

This response is aroused by any number of objects: the fine spring night; the "velvety lilac texture" of the sky, "glittering with great stars"; the streets outside the theatre crowded with hansoms; New York in an intoxicating earlier era; DeWolfe Hopper, the actor, running around "pretending to be a horse and neighing, and trying to climb up a lamppost"; the old car itself with "its rich wine color, its great polished lamps of brass . . . and all its wonderful and exciting smells." These make up a rich compost of external detail, strategically drawn from both society and nature. No wonder the narrator exclaims: "Everyone seemed to be as happy and elated as we were, it seemed as if a new world and new people had burst out of the earth with the coming of spring. . . . I saw all of it, I felt myself a part of it all, I wanted to possess it all."

But the story is something more than a simple exercise in romantic enthusiasm. It is kept from soaring off into the blue by the somber presence of death. Death in two forms: as a premonition and as an actuality. On two occasions, near the beginning and just before the end, the girl mentions the fact that it all took place the year before her father died. And on a third occasion, as they enter the park and feel the first rush of ecstatic pleasure in their new surroundings, she looks at her father and suddenly knows that he is going to die. This so heightens her feelings and so sharpens her perceptions that the lengthy final paragraph of the story records in great detail and with scientific precision the exact cries of the numerous birds at dawn.

Her premonition of her father's approaching death escalates her appreciation of life and her sensory response to it. The intrusion of death jolts us but at the same time intensifies our awareness of life's familiar attractions. The birds break into their chorus every morning, though we usually pay little attention to them. By compelling our attention, death becomes an agent of life and is thus absorbed into the story's inner flow.

The naturalness and skill with which the tale is put together are revealed in the opening lines. The narrator gropes in her mind and memory to get back to that magic evening long years ago. For a few sentences she slides about uncertainly: "That year I think we were living with Bella; no, we weren't, I guess we were living with Auntie Kate—well, maybe we were staying with Bella: I don't know, we moved around so much, and it's so long ago. It gets all confused in my mind now." Then the fog of time miraculously lifts and suddenly everything is in the clear. The evening in question detaches itself from its murky background and glistens into focus. In this way, proceeding from confusion to clarity, one enters the story.

One exits from it along the same path, only in the reverse direction, from the spellbinding clarity of the bird songs to confusion and uncertainty again as memory begins to lapse. "That was the year before he died and I think we were staying at Bella's then, but maybe we were staying at the old hotel, or perhaps we had already moved to Auntie Kate's: we moved around so much, we lived in so many places, it seems so long ago, that when I try to think about it now it gets confused and I cannot remember."

This refrain at the end illustrates the familiar operation of memory. It also supplies "In The Park" with a band or circle of cottony haze inside which lies preserved and intact, like some magically propertied jewel, the briefly caught but blazingly lucid glimpse of an earlier time and place.

The same process on a larger, more complex scale is seen at work in "The Lost Boy," the second of Wolfe's superb short stories. This appeared in *The Hills Beyond*, the last of the books Edward Aswell assembled after the author's death. It deals with the death in boyhood of Grover, Ben Gant's twin, during the St. Louis World's Fair of 1904.

Divided into four parts, each told from a different point of view, the story is an intricate attempt to make tragedy coherent. Grover's death from typhoid fever is cruel, unexpected, and sudden. It has a shattering effect on everyone there: on his sister Helen who had gone about town with him on that last day; on his mother, whose passion for profit had brought them to St. Louis in the first place; on Eugene, only four at the time but already conscious of the tragedy which aroused in him feelings and vibrations he would be unable to explain until many years later. The story conveys the shock of death but equally the effort to absorb the shock, recover from it, and eventually conquer it.

Part One begins with Grover back home in Altamont, standing in front of Mr. Crocker's shop in the town square, greedily contemplating the freshly made candy in the window. The temptation is too strong. He enters, buys the candy, pays Mr. Crocker—a mean, spiteful figure out of

Dickens—in stamps, is cheated on the change. Burning with injustice, he rushes across the street to his father, who invades the Crocker premises, gets Grover's money back, and helps his son through a small painful crisis in his young life. In the deliberate chronology of the four parts, the first starts with the father, the source and the beginning in the biological scheme of things.

Part Two shifts to the mother. With her narration, Grover passes into the minds of others. In Part One he had appeared directly and in his own person before us, the one occasion that he was wholly alive and himself. Then, as a fore-shadowing of his approaching death, he loses his status as an independent, self-contained being and begins his existence in the consciousness of those around him. Beginning with his mother, whose thoughts contain everything of Grover's life and death.

She remembers the trip to St. Louis, with the train bowling along the Indiana countryside. She remembers Grover, now twelve, working at the Fair, how good he was at shopping and bargaining, what a grave, serious, disciplined, intelligent boy he had already become. She remembers the lacerating impact of his dying, a wound that continued to bleed within her for an endless time.

She never forgets Grover. Years later, after Eugene has become a celebrated writer, a scholar came South in quest of information about him. She remembers how surprised he was when she told him that Grover had been smarter than Eugene, and in saying that and thinking it, she finds Grover becoming more vividly fixed in her memory than ever. Thus Grover's life appears in two sections, before and after death. The section before death is the shorter one, and is exceeded in both length and power by the lucidity and vibrancy of his psychological continuation in the thoughts of his survivors. The story is of course about life and death, but it is also about immortality. Grover's posthumous existence outlives his mortal one.

The speaker of Part Three is Helen, sister and next in the biological progression of "The Lost Boy." She brings us the voice of someone much closer to Grover in age than his father and mother. But she is still older than he, old enough to feel the full brunt of his death, to feel it as something ghastly and inexplicable. Now deep into her adult life, she still cannot accommodate herself to it. How could it have happened? she asks Eugene. Why is the world filled with stupid empty people who go on living while someone as fine as Grover is cut down so young? To these familiar, conventional questions she has no answer.

Helen remembers how on that last afternoon Grover had decided to spend his pay on a treat instead of dutifully bringing it home. The two of them had gone into a cheap eatery and gorged themselves on pork and beans. After all this time, she remembers the sense of liberation the "treat" had given them. And not a moment too soon, for no sooner had they gotten home, even before Grover had a chance to be properly scolded, he came down with his sudden fatal fever, and by the next day was gone. For the rest of her life Helen was distraught and baffled by the tragedy. Grover's legacy to her was a deep groove of angry bewilderment from which she was destined never to recover.

Finally, in Part Four, we come to Eugene, the youngest of the narrators. He was present when Grover died but was too young at the time to understand fully what was going on. His response, necessarily delayed, comes later, more than thirty years later in fact, and Part Four is an account of Eugene's return to St. Louis in the 1930s in search of his lost brother. He goes back to the street where they lived during the Fair, searches out the house they occupied, which miraculously is still standing, and makes his way to the very bedroom where Grover fell ill and died. None of this is easy. The city has changed, the street is not as it was, and the present owner of the house is a stranger who proves accommodating only after Eugene explains to her, not without awkwardness, what he is after.

What he is after is not wholly clear to himself. It somehow seems terrifically important that he recapture and reoccupy the original scene. By reliving Grover's death, perhaps he can exorcise it, lay it to rest, quiet and settle the spirit of his brother so prematurely lost. But he is also moved by the opposite impulse. In getting Grover to die again, this time in his mind's eye, he will absorb the event into himself in a way that he was too young to do the first time. The quest for Grover is a quest for emotional understanding.

Grover's passing must not only be witnessed, it must also be felt. It is the emotion that triumphs over death, so that Eugene's search for the emotion aroused by the original catastrophe is in some obscure way a search for life. The story reaches its final intention at this point. Man does conquer death: by feeling it in all its horror, awfulness, and pain he absorbs it into himself, and thus survives. As Grover survives, in the clarity and strength of the feelings engendered by his terrifying departure in those around him.

The climactic nature of Part Four begins to emerge. Because he was so young when Grover died, Eugene is the only figure who must voluntarily, and with an immense effort of the will, engage himself in the reenactment of the tragedy. The others—Eliza, Helen—involuntarily caught up in it as captive and compelled witnesses, were able to experience it at the time.

In going back to the place of Grover's departure, Eugene relives not only Grover's death but Grover himself. The lost boy is never so real as when he is on the abrupt verge of being snatched away. If that moment can be fixed, preserved, sealed off from time, memorialized, kept intact, then Grover cannot be reduced and is ours forever.

So Eugene obscurely reasons, or perhaps only obscurely feels. The story is a supreme episode in Wolfe's relentless quest for immortality. The search for Grover is also a search for the secret process by which the human can be saved from the dissolution of time and the laxness of memory. Wolfe was a fervent, lifelong pursuer of these matters, and "The Lost Boy" is one of his great demonstrations in the art of robbing death to shore up life.

7

The Novelist Who Got Away

👑👑 In the Foreword to this book eight clichés about Wolfe were listed. How true are they?

1. Were Wolfe's novels autobiographical? Only at first, and progressively less so as they went along. He wrote about the lives of the rich and the poor, though he belonged to neither. He projected the character of persons strikingly different from himself and of events outside his own particular experience. He perceptively analyzed cities and countries that were not his own. He dealt with historical movements and philosophies of human conduct that, far from applying to him personally, belonged to the age as a whole. And toward the end of his life he was planning an immense series of books dealing with those earlier generations of Americans that were quite plainly outside the orbit of his own life.

2. Did he ever develop emotionally beyond late adolescence? It is hard to read a story like "The Lost Boy," written in 1937 near the very end of his career, without an intimate sense of being in the presence of a mature and responsible consciousness. The same is true of "In The Park," "Chickamauga," "Gentlemen of the Press," "No Door," "The Four Lost Men," "Gulliver," "The Bums at Sunset," "The Far and the Near," and "The Men of Old Catawba." These stories are of varying quality, but none centers around the "I," none is an expression of the romantic ego, and all are obviously the work of a writer who, in his art at any rate, has outgrown adolescence.

While the record is not so conclusive in the novels, even there the tone struck at various points—Ben's death in *Look Homeward, Angel,* the satirical account of the budding playwrights and plays in Professor Hatcher's class at Harvard, the tragic chronicle of Dick Prosser, Mr. and Mrs. Jack waking up and sliding into their respective routines, the portrait of Lloyd McHarg, the outpouring of conscience in the final letter to Foxhall Edwards—is remarkably, inescapably, that of a man who has fully grown up.

3. Were his works just miscellaneous outpourings and not really organized works of art? That, of course, is everyone's first reaction. First impressions of Wolfe are highly dangerous since his surface is so flashy and volatile. All that energy, enthusiasm, and eloquent verbal rush come at one with overwhelming force. If the reader can recover from the initial impression and explore what lies beneath it, he is likely to emerge with a radically different perspective. There is an unsuspected amount of evidence indicating that Wolfe knew what he was doing, that he planned his effects carefully, at times even painstakingly, and that, like Faulkner who so greatly admired him, he had the overall plan for his books worked out before he began writing them.

This was the contention of Edward Aswell who, as his editor, worked closely with Wolfe during the last two years of his life. And it is evident from Wolfe's notebooks, in the two volumes of them edited by Richard S. Kennedy and Paschal Reeves, that the process of alteration, revision, recasting, reconstruction—all the difficult stages from the time an idea is conceived to its final form—went on all the time. The wonder is that with so much of this taking place he was able to create the effect of spontaneity, of almost scattershot immediacy, even of artlessness which from the start were thought to be his exclusive qualities.

4. Was Wolfe so derivative, did he owe so much to his predecessors that little or no room remained for originality of his own? It is true that his debt to Keats and Shelley, to Rabelais and Joyce—among others—is highly visible, is never really shaken off and left behind. Like his mother, he was a great hoarder, not of pieces of string but of literary materials. He was loath to give anything up, a memory, a sense perception, an influence, any idea however outworn. Once Keats, with his obsessive longing for fame and immortality, got into Wolfe's bloodstream, he was there forever; Wolfe would never release him. And so with everything.

Yet out of the immense compost heap of influences, out of the huge grab bag of assorted impressions and experiences, Wolfe did create at least two things that were entirely, originally his own. One was his feeling for life—an open-faced, naïve, unabashed, enthusiastic commitment that permeates every line he ever wrote. Traces of the same attitude appear in other writers, but seldom in so pure or intense a form. Wolfe's other notable achievement was his sense of art, which imposed radical changes on his own work and compelled him, after his more or less traditional debut, to find new avenues for his energy. His later novels are indifferent examples of conventional fiction, but profoundly interesting examples of novels on the way to developing into something else, into deliberately timeless and fixated representations of experience. Wolfe turned out to be astonishingly original both in his attitude toward the life materials which fed his art and to the progressing forms of that art itself.

5. Can the psychology of his life and work be summed up as a search for the lost father? The need for a strong older figure was certainly there, but it proved no more powerful than its opposite impulse: the need to break free of the senior influence and stand on one's own. Wolfe's biography can be read as a struggle between these two influences.

Of the two, the impulse toward freedom and independence was plainly triumphant. After the quarrel with Perkins, Wolfe was entirely his own man, and during the last years of his life seems to have felt no need for still another human rock on which to anchor himself. And his last book, *You Can't Go Home Again,* can be read as the chronicle of George Webber finally disengaging himself from all those sources of outside strength to which he had originally been drawn: Mrs. Jack, the German fatherland, Foxhall Edwards. Wolfe's career is as much a process of getting rid of the father figure as it is a search to find one.

6. Was his one dimension gigantism? Was he indeed obsessed with size, bulk, and quantity? No one would have any trouble amassing numerous passages to support this impression. A closer reading of Wolfe's work, however, reveals his talent as a miniaturist, side by side with and

perhaps as a counterweight to his inflationary style.

He will often isolate some small moment, some tiny detail, and concentrate on its smallness with the same almost compulsive passion with which he will blow up certain already large emotions and landscapes beyond life size. His energies flow as naturally and fluently into a small space as into a large. He oscillates from one dimension to the other, seldom pausing for anything in between. The territory of moderation is not for him. He crosses it as rapidly as possible, hell-bent in one or another of his favorite directions. But his zest for the tiny is as pronounced as his appetite for the huge.

7. Was he in truth weighted down, if not actually crippled, by vicious prejudices, racial and otherwise? They were certainly vicious enough, not only with regard to those two perennially familiar targets in America, Jews and Negroes, but toward the whole range of European immigrant groups, with the poor whites in the South and the mass population of Northern cities thrown in for good measure. Wolfe never did anything by halves. When he hated or detested or derided or held in contempt—as when he admired and loved—he committed himself to the project wholly. It is foolish, as well as pointless, to play down his anti-Semitism by claiming, as some have, that it was more verbal than emotional, just a manner of speaking as it were. Aline Bernstein did not think so, and she was in a strategic position to know.

How far his prejudices ate into his art is more difficult to decide. Our liberal inclination is to deny genius to writers with reactionary opinions or racially bigoted attitudes, to disqualify them in some way as a sign of our disapproval, or at the very least to criticize them severely in our minds. From this point of view there are a great many authentic geniuses to be censured, if not actually banned. Gogol, Dostoevsky, and T. S. Eliot were ferocious anti-Semites. Yeats, Pound, and Céline were unblinking fascists. Nietzsche and Balzac despised democracy and the democratic process. The attitude toward Negroes of Conrad and Faulkner was anything but enlightened.

Whether this weakened their art is moot. The intensity of even their regressive convictions might just as easily have served as a source of potency and strength. On this mysterious subject it is difficult to draw any hard and fast conclusions. Wolfe's prejudices have no doubt offended most of his admirers as they have provided his detractors with explosive ammunition against him. But whether they were a destructive force in his writing is almost impossible to determine.

8. Was he powerfully obsessed by time? Undoubtedly. But it was an obsession that he learned to deal with. In the struggle between art and time—from his viewpoint a struggle between life and death—art had the strength to impose itself on time and, by rescuing experience from time's destructive and annihilating oblivion, check its destructive power. Wolfe began by fearing it was all in vain, that the past could not be rescued, that memory was too fallible and art too finite. But after years of increasing effort, training his memory to evoke the past as arduously and in as disciplined a way as Freud trained himself to recall his own dreams, he developed it into an instrument tempered to his purposes.

What memory evoked, art preserved. If Wolfe became a worshipper of art, as were Keats, Flaubert, and Joyce before him, it was because art revealed itself to him as the only process available to men that could conquer time. Once this revelation came to him—and it came as the result of his own consuming labors—his fear of time was overcome. To be cured of such a fear, equivalent to the fear of death itself, led to a certain maturity of outlook, even a certain serenity of soul conspicuously absent in the early Wolfe and surprisingly manifest in the later one.

If the record of his art was a search for new forms of expression, the record of his life was a remorseless pursuit of control over his own past, which meant in the end a control over himself. He was not absolutely successful in either. But he was successful to a considerable degree.

Soon after Wolfe's death, Edward Aswell, assembling *The Hills Beyond,* raised a fundamental question, but did not answer it satisfactorily. Then the question lapsed and has not been dealt with adequately since. "If one tries to judge his works by the conventional standards of the novel," Aswell wrote, "one is licked at the start." If this statement were applied to the work after *Look Homeward, Angel,* it would be profoundly true. By including the first novel, Aswell missed the great change in Wolfe's direction. "Wolfe is supposed to have written novels," he went on to observe. "Wolfe's books are not like that. . . . So what in the name of God are they?"

What indeed? They are like life, Aswell says. They have the form of life itself. Aside from the vagueness of the word "life" in this context, one is moved to say that Wolfe's books are not at all like "life." They are instead an extraordinary idealization of life, exhibiting those qualities of emotional resonance, sensuous vitality, and the quest for the permanent, the enduring, and the eternal that we long for in life but seldom find.

Wolfe remains a peculiarly American treasure. All those traits that used to be associated with America—exuberance, energy, naïveté, a longing for success and admiration, wrapped inside a shell of persistent idealism, an obstinate tendency to concentrate on the best and worst without bothering with anything between—were abundantly and extravagantly his.

Unlike his famous contemporaries, he made no attempt to protect or disguise himself. Fitzgerald hid his bruised heart and disillusioned spirit behind a screen of rueful irony. Hemingway kept his internal bleeding under control by training himself to be toughminded; when the training process broke down, *he* broke down. Faulkner managed to bear the tragedy of the present by making frequent excursions into the past. By contrast, Wolfe made no attempt to mask his feelings, instead gave vent to them with uncompromising candor. In an age whose expression was elliptical, whose strategy was indirection, whose reigning belief was that everything was a symbol or an emblem of something else, Wolfe stands out as a remarkable embodiment of eager straightforwardness and literal honesty.

He thought of himself as a performer of miracles. He would go forth and conquer the earth, become universally famous, master life, make time stand still, transcend mortality. He was not wholly triumphant in any of these matchless endeavors, but he did not wholly fail in any of them either. He embraced a supreme function of the artist: to serve as scout for the rest of us, to carry out reconnaissance in uncharted and hence dangerous territory without which no general advance is possible. In this sense, his life as a writer was a supreme adventure, pursued with unflagging ardor and unstinting devotion. Whatever their shortcomings as individual works, whatever their obvious defects, his books are massive and unassailable milestones along the path of that adventure.

By breaking free or the format of the novel in his own

special fashion, he became the novelist who got away, and thus forged for himself an instrument by which the exploration of life in terms of its ultimate possibilities could be sustained. A certain greatness of spirit has always been associated with the American dream. Wolfe makes his appeal to us in terms of that greatness and registers for us with intimate finality our sense of, our feeling for, the country which produced him and nurtures us.

A Selected Bibliography

The three principal collections of Wolfe materials—manuscripts, letters, family papers, memorabilia, first editions—are at Harvard, the University of North Carolina, and the Pack Memorial Library, Asheville, North Carolina. I am indebted to James Meehan for his friendly assistance on my visit to Asheville.

BY WOLFE

FICTION

Look Homeward, Angel. New York: Charles Scribner's Sons, 1929.

Of Time and the River. New York: Charles Scribner's Sons, 1935.

From Death to Morning. New York: Charles Scribner's Sons, 1935.

The Web and the Rock. New York: Harper and Brothers, 1939.

You Can't Go Home Again. New York: Harper and Brothers, 1940.

The Hills Beyond. New York: Harper and Brothers, 1941.

The Short Novels of Thomas Wolfe, ed. C. Hugh Holman. New York: Charles Scribner's Sons, 1961.

NONFICTION

The Story of a Novel. New York: Charles Scribner's Sons, 1936.

"A Western Journey," *Virginia Quarterly Review,* Summer 1939.

Thomas Wolfe's Letters to His Mother, ed. John Skally Terry. New York: Charles Scribner's Sons, 1943.

The Correspondence of Thomas Wolfe and Homer Andrew Watt, eds. Oscar Cargill and Thomas C. Pollock. New York: New York University Press, 1954.

The Letters of Thomas Wolfe, ed. Elizabeth Nowell. New York: Charles Scribner's Sons, 1956.

Thomas Wolfe's Purdue Speech: "Writing and Living," eds. William Braswell and Leslie A. Field. Lafayette, Ind.: Purdue University Studies, 1964.

The Notebooks of Thomas Wolfe, eds. Richard S. Kennedy and Paschal Reeves. Chapel Hill, N.C.: University of North Carolina Press, 1969. 2 vols.

The Mountains, ed. Pat M. Ryan. Chapel Hill, N.C.: University of North Carolina Press, 1970. Wolfe's play, in both the one-act and three-act versions.

ABOUT WOLFE

Bernstein, Aline. "Eugene." *Three Blue Suits.* New York: Equinox Cooperative Press, 1933. A short story describing her relationship with Wolfe.

————. *The Journey Down.* New York: Alfred A. Knopf, 1938.

Cowley, Malcolm. *A Second Flowering: Works and Days of the Lost Generation.* New York: Viking Press, 1973. Contains a significant chapter on Wolfe, "Wolfe *Homo Scribens.*"

Field, Leslie A., ed. *Thomas Wolfe: Three Decades of Criticism.* New York: New York University Press, 1968.

Holman, C. Hugh, ed. *The World of Thomas Wolfe*. New York: Charles Scribner's Sons, 1962.

Johnson, Elmer D. *Thomas Wolfe: A Checklist*. Kent, Ohio: The Kent State University Press, 1970.

Johnson, Pamela Hansford. *Hungry Gulliver: An English Critical Appraisal of Thomas Wolfe*. New York: Charles Scribner's Sons, 1948.

Kennedy, Richard S. *The Window of Memory: The Literary Career of Thomas Wolfe*. Chapel Hill, N.C.: University of North Carolina Press, 1962.

McCoy, George W. "Asheville and Thomas Wolfe," *North Carolina Historical Review*, XXX (April 1953), 200–217.

Modern Fiction Studies, Autumn 1965. A special number devoted to Wolfe, with a checklist of criticism on his work.

Muller, Herbert J. *Thomas Wolfe*. Makers of Modern Literature Series. Norfolk, Conn.: New Directions, 1947.

Norwood, Hayden. *The Marble Man's Wife: Thomas Wolfe's Mother*. New York: Charles Scribner's Sons, 1947.

Nowell, Elizabeth. *Thomas Wolfe: A Biography*. Garden City, N.Y.: Doubleday, 1960.

Pollock, Thomas C., and Oscar Cargill. *Thomas Wolfe at Washington Square*. New York: New York University Press, 1954.

Reeves, Paschal. *Thomas Wolfe's Albatross: Race and Nationality in America*. Athens, Ga.: University of Georgia Press, 1968.

Rubin, Louis D., Jr. *Thomas Wolfe: The Weather of His Youth*. Baton Rouge, La.: Louisiana State University Press, 1955.

Turnbull, Andrew. *Thomas Wolfe*. New York: Charles Scribner's Sons, 1967. A critical biography.

Walser, Richard, ed. *The Enigma of Thomas Wolfe: Biographical and Critical Selections*. Cambridge, Mass.: Harvard University Press, 1953.

Wheaton, Mabel Wolfe, and LeGette Blythe. *Thomas Wolfe and His Family*. Garden City, N.Y.: Doubleday, 1961.

Index

Anderson, Sherwood, 50, 90
"Angel on the Porch, An," 31
Asheville (North Carolina), 5, 9, 10, 14, 34–35, 43, 46, 139, 144
Aswell, Edward C., 3, 42, 80, 84n, 163, 169, 173

Baker, George Pierce, 4, 16, 20, 21–22
Bernstein, Aline, 4–5, 26–30, 31, 32, 34, 104, 121, 172
Boyd, Madeleine, 30, 40

Carnera, Primo, 3
"Chickamauga" *(The Hills Beyond)*, 7, 159, 169
Conrad, Joseph, 120, 172

"Death of Ivan Ilyich, The" (Tolstoy), 93

De Voto, Bernard, 39–40, 86, 87
Dos Passos, John, 16, 83–84, 130
Dreiser, Theodore, 77, 107

Faulkner, William, 16, 26, 169, 172, 174
Fitzgerald, F. Scott, 16, 26, 31, 32–33, 48, 119, 174
Forster, E. M., 134
From Death to Morning, 40, 160

Germany, 6, 33, 38, 41, 99
Grapes of Wrath, The (Steinbeck), 146, 154–157
"Gulliver" *(From Death to Morning)*, 5, 131, 169
Gulliver's Travels (Swift), 130–131

Hemingway, Ernest, 3, 16, 26, 31, 32, 109, 126, 174

181

Hills Beyond, The, 163, 173

"In The Park" *(From Death to Morning),* 7, 160–163, 169

James, Henry, 3, 12, 80, 101
Jews, 5, 6, 25, 41, 96–97, 118, 171–172
Joyce, James, 3–4, 5, 60–61, 64, 66, 74, 77, 83, 117, 130, 170, 173

Keats, John, 3, 65, 83, 170, 173
Koch, Frederick, 15–16

Lardner, Ring, 26, 31
Lawrence, D. H., 53, 77
Lewis, Sinclair, 26, 33–34, 77, 145
Look Homeward, Angel, 4, 14, 27, 28–29, 31–33, 34, 37, 38, 40, 41, 45, 47, 49–77, 79, 81, 85, 94, 102, 108, 109, 114, 130, 136, 137, 144, 153, 169, 173
"Lost Boy, The" *(The Hills Beyond),* 12, 163–167, 168–169
"Lycidas" (Milton), 32, 50

Manhattan Transfer (Dos Passos), 83
Middletown (Robert and Helen Lynd), 140
Milton, John, 32, 50, 74

Nazis, 6, 33, 38, 41
Negroes, 5, 6, 171
Nostromo (Conrad), 120–121
Nowell, Elizabeth, 42

Of Time and the River, 21, 25, 33, 37, 38, 39, 41, 47, 79–107, 114, 118, 130, 132, 139, 144
O'Neill, Eugene, 107

Perkins, Maxwell E., 3, 4, 30–31, 32, 35, 36, 37–38, 40, 41–43, 44, 80, 85–86, 87, 106, 139, 153, 171
Plato, 87, 134–135

Rabelais, François, 125, 130, 170
Raisbeck, Kenneth, 22–23, 26
Roberts, Margaret, 13–14, 15, 20, 22, 34

Scribner's Sons, Charles, 3, 30, 31, 38, 40–41, 42
Shakespeare, William, 38, 74
Shelley, Percy Bysshe, 3, 170
Steinbeck, John, 155–157
Story of a Novel, The, 39, 105–106
Styron, William, 2
Swift, Jonathan, 5, 130–131

time, 6, 106, 152, 172–173
"To Autumn" (Keats), 65
Tolstoy, Count Leo, 93
Twain, Mark, 3

Ulysses (Joyce), 4, 5, 60, 66
Utrillo, Maurice, 81

Web and the Rock, The, 7, 42, 45, 47, 108–136, 144, 148
"Web of Earth, The" *(From Death to Morning),* 159

Westall, Henry, 21
Whitman, Walt, 3, 107
Winesburg, Ohio (Anderson), 140
Wolfe, Benjamin Harrison, 11, 12–13, 16–17, 45
Wolfe, Frank, 11–12
Wolfe, Fred, 13, 16
Wolfe, Grover Cleveland, 11, 12, 45
Wolfe, Julia Westall, 9–11, 14, 18–20
Wolfe, Mabel, 12, 16, 44
Wolfe, Thomas: appearance, 14, 17, 27, 36; in Brooklyn, 34, 35–36; early years in North

Wolfe, Thomas (*cont.*)
Carolina, 13–17; in Europe, 25–26, 28–29, 30, 33, 41; family relations, 9–13; final illness and death, 43–45; at Harvard, 20–23; at New York University, 24–25, 29; temperament, 19–20, 23, 27; writing habits, 17, 36–38
Wolfe, W. O., 4, 9–11, 15, 16, 17–18, 20, 45
Wordsworth, William, 56, 83

You Can't Go Home Again, 42, 47, 84, 98, 116, 130, 135, 137–158, 171

ABOUT THE AUTHOR

Leo Gurko was for many years professor of English at Hunter College in New York, and from 1954 to 1960 served as chairman of the department. He is currently the John Cranford Adams Professor of English Literature at Hofstra University in Hempstead, Long Island, where he teaches both graduate and undergraduate courses in twentieth-century literature. He received his B.A. from the College of the City of Detroit and his M.A. and Ph.D. from the University of Wisconsin.

Among his published books are *Tom Paine, Freedom's Apostle, The Two Lives of Joseph Conrad,* and *Ernest Hemingway and the Pursuit of Heroism.* He has written many articles on modern English and American literature, particularly on Joseph Conrad, D. H. Lawrence, and Ernest Hemingway. A number of these have been frequently reprinted, and several have appeared in French and Italian translations. Dr. Gurko has also worked as a publisher's reader, editor, and translator. He has made frequent radio and television appearances.

He enjoys playing tennis, going to the movies, traveling, and following professional baseball. He has spent three separate years in Europe, one with his family on a grant from the Ford Foundation and the other two on sabbatical leave. His son is an attorney in Denver, his daughter an associate professor of English at California State College, San Francisco. He and his wife, herself an author of biographies and histories for young people, divide their time between their apartment in New York City and their house in the country fifty miles away.

DATE			